CONTENTS

MAKING A SMALL CLAIM IN THE COUNTY

COURT

The Easyway

Peter Jarrett

Editor Roger Sproston

Easyway Guides

British Cataloguing in Publication data. A catalogue record is available for this book from the British Library.

ISBN
978-1-913776-11-4

Printed in the United Kingdom by 4edge www.4edge.co.uk
Cover Design by Straightforward Graphics

Chapter 1.

Introduction to Making a Small Claim

The aim of this guide, which is intended to be for the layperson as opposed to the professional, is to explain the procedure by which you can bring or defend a small claim and how to enforce a judgment. This guide is a guide to procedure not a précis on "the law" or "your rights".

The small claims procedure has evolved over the years, initially limited to claims involving sums in dispute of not more than £100. However, over the years that limit has increased and now stands at £10,000 for money claims (£3,000 in Scotland and £3,000 in Northern Ireland). Readers should be aware that, when it comes to claims against local authorities however, you have to apply for a judicial review to the High Court. If you do not, they can apply to strike out and you will have to pay their solicitors costs. Tread carefully here!

Small claims and the Pandemic
Small claims, like all other aspects of the court system, have been impacted by Covid-19 in terms of timeliness, official figures have shown. In July to September 2020, it took an average of 48.8 weeks between a small claim being issued and the claim going to trial, 10.7 weeks longer than the same period in 2019.

For multi- and fast-track claims, it took on average 62 weeks to reach a trial, 2.6 weeks longer than in July to September 2019 –

continuing to exceed the upper limit of the range over the past decade of 52 to 61 weeks.

Overall, the impact of Covid-19 continued to be seen across all civil justice. While the MoJ said "the start of recovery has been noticeable", for example in the volume of claims and defences, "this increase has been gradual and volumes are still below previous years".

Therefore, at the moment, expect a small claim application to take that much longer in 2021.

This book covers England and Wales and for advice on Scotland the reader should go to www.scotcourts.gov.uk/taking-action/small-claims.

For Northern Ireland www.nidirect.gov.uk/articles/small-claims-process.

Every year, more than 100,000 small claims are commenced in the county court. The Civil Procedure Rules guide small claims and they ensure that a consistent approach to the resolution of small claims is adopted across the board. Prior to 2000, there was no appeal against an award in a small claims court. However, since October of that year there has been a full appeal procedure which is the same as for other cases governed by the Civil Procedure Rules.

Terminology

A definition of legal terms is contained within the glossary of the book. The Civil Procedure Rules created a new terminology for litigation. The person bringing the case is known as the 'Claimant'. Virtually all small claims cases are dealt with by district judges, save for the few that are dealt with by Circuit Judges at the time of an appeal. All county courts will deal with small claims cases and there is no separate building or court called the 'small claims' court. Nearly all hearings are conducted in the normal county court building, usually in a room containing the litigants and the judge. Mediations are held under the auspices of the National Mediation Helpline 0800 246 1218 and are often held in local solicitors offices, the parties homes or offices or some other agreed venue.

Small claims tracks

The three management categories for civil claims in the county court are called 'tracks'.

They are shown overleaf:

Small claims track Part 27	Cases up to £10,000 in value except:
	Cases which include a claim for personal injury up to £1,000 in value only
	Housing cases-limited to where the claim against the landlord is for repair/damages no more than £1,000 each
Fast Track part 28	Cases above the small claims limit but of no more than £25,000 in value and where the case can be heard in one day or less.
Multi-track part29	Cases which do not qualify for the small claims or fast track including all cases over £25,000 in value.

The small claims track provides a simple and informal way of resolving disputes and should enable you to dispense with the services of a lawyer. The amount in dispute should normally be less than £10,000. A person can ask for a claim to be dealt with in the small claims track if the amount is more than £10,000 but the defendant must agree with the suggestion and a judge must be satisfied that the case is simple enough for the small claims track. If the claim for over £10,000 is dealt with in the small claims track then the winner can claim all costs against the losing party. These costs, however, can be no more than those that would have been awarded in the fast track. Normally, the person who wins the case cannot normally recover their solicitors' fees from their opponent other than the fixed costs on the issue of the Claim Form, witness and other expenses. Costs are explained in Chapter 15. For allocation to the 'fast-track' the claim will be between £10,000 and £25,000. The fast track is for cases that can be resolved in one day or less. If a judge deems that the case should be allocated to the multi-track, because it is over £25,000 or is too complex this will be communicated to the claimant. If the claim is allocated to the multi-track then advice should be sought from a solicitor. Although you may well be able to present the case in court the amount of preparatory work can be daunting.

With fast and Multi track cases costs can be awarded up to the value of 2/3 of the costs on average.

The court will send you a notice of which track the case has been allocated to. If it has been allocated to the fast-track then form N154 will be sent to you together with instructions as to what you need to do to prepare for trial, called 'directions'. If the claim has been allocated to the multi-track then form N155 will be sent. Standard directions and a typical timetable for a fast track case will be:

- Disclosure of documents (followed by inspection) four weeks after allocation
- Exchange of witness statements-10 weeks
- Exchange of expert reports (where appropriate) -14 weeks
- Court send out listing questionnaire -20 weeks
- Return questionnaire -22 weeks
- Trial – around 30 weeks.

For multi-track cases, there is no standard procedure, each case will be managed according to its complexity. A case management conference may be held, where the judge gets together with all the parties to review the progress of the case. Small claims are heard in the county courts by the district judge. The person who is bringing the claim is called the "claimant" and the person he is making the claim against is known as the "defendant". When a hearing has taken place the district judge will reach a decision known as a "judgment". This is a court order, which usually requires certain actions such as to pay compensation or "damages" to the claimant or the claim will be dismissed if the defendant is successful.

*****

Chapter 2.

Types of Small Claim in the County Court

This chapter reviews the types of claim that could fall under the small claims track. Small claims most often result from a breach of contract such as non-payment of an invoice, or breach of express or implied terms, or can result from circumstances where there is no contract like personal injury (known as "tort"), or for non-payment of a cheque.

The Supplier's Contractual Rights to Payment- Express term

Where goods are delivered or services rendered, the supplier or service provider is entitled to the agreed price or agreed payment for the service rendered. If no price has been agreed, the supplier or service provider is entitled to a reasonable sum for the goods supplied or service rendered.

Breach of Contract: Purchaser's Rights

When goods are supplied which do not comply with the contract, or in breach of terms implied by the Sale of Goods Act (see below), the purchaser is entitled to either:-

- Compensation known as "damages", or
- If the breach is serious, to reject the goods and claim damages for financial loss, for example, a refund of the purchase price, or the cost above the agreed purchase price for goods within the terms of contract, and any additional loss suffered. The compensation claimed

would be the purchase price and any other additional loss suffered. In this situation, the contract is discharged, which means that the purchaser is released of his obligation of payment, or

- To reject the goods and affirm the contract, which means that the contract is not discharged and the purchaser requires the supplier to perform the contract and holds the supplier to his contractual obligation. If the contract is not performed, the aggrieved party may sue for breach of contract

- Section 75 of the Consumer Credit Act 1974 allows the same "purchasers' rights" to be enforced against a credit card company when the goods are purchased by credit card when the balance can be carried forward from month to month. The same rule does not apply to debit cards.

Sale of Goods Act, 1979- Implied Terms

The Sale of Goods Act 1979 has now been replaced by the Consumer Rights Act 2015 (see below), but you may be able to claim under it if the goods you bought were purchased on or before 30th September 2015, and became faulty. The Sale of Goods Act implies certain terms into contracts for the sale of goods. This means that the seller must supply goods, which satisfy certain statutory terms of contract imposed by Parliament. The principal implied terms are:-

- The vendor must own the goods or have the right to sell them

- If the goods are sold by description they must correspond with that description.

- This applies to goods which are described in some way by a label or a notice identifying the kind of goods they are, or to specific goods which the buyer has not seen at the time of the contract and which are bought on the basis of a description. Where a seller sells goods in the course of a business the goods must be of satisfactory quality. This is defined as meaning that they must meet the standard that a reasonable person would regard as satisfactory, taking account of any description of the goods, the price (if relevant) and all the other relevant circumstances. The Act lists the following as aspects of the quality of goods; the fitness for the purpose for which goods of the kind in questions are commonly supplied, the appearance and finish, freedom from minor defects, safety and durability. These provisions do not apply to goods of unsatisfactory quality if fault has been specifically drawn to the buyer's attention before the contract is made
- If the goods are sold by the bulk must correspond to the sample in quality and be free from any defect which would not be apparent on reasonable examination of the sample.

If these conditions are not satisfied, the purchaser has the rights specified above, to damages, to rejection and damages, or to affirm the contract and claim damages for loss suffered.

Consumer Rights Act 2015

As mentioned, this Act replaced The Sales of Goods Act 1979 for goods purchased after 30th September 2015. The Act relates to the supply of services, which includes a vast range of activities, from having your house altered or redecorated, to having your hair dyed, to having your coat dry cleaned. It includes the supply of goods because often when services are supplied with materials, the materials must be of a suitable quality.

The supplier of services is entitled to payment of his invoice and if a price has not been agreed he is entitled to a reasonable charge. Even if the work is not a reasonable standard the supplier may be entitled to a reasonable payment.

Where someone acting in the course of a business supplies a service, the purchaser is entitled to receive a service performed with reasonable care and skill and carried out within a reasonable time. If goods are supplied they must be of satisfactory quality and correspond to any description or sample by which they have been sold. If the work or goods are not of a reasonable standard the purchaser must prove that this is the case and may claim the remedies mentioned above. For example a purchaser may be entitled to damages if the work is so substandard that financial loss is suffered such as for plumbing or re-wiring which needs to be completely re-done or a coat, which needs to be replaced after cleaning.

The Consumer Rights Act 2015 also applies to contracts for the hire of goods although not to hire purchase agreements. Like contracts for sale, contracts for hire have terms implied into them that the supplier of the goods (the bailor) has the right to hire them out, that they correspond to any description or sample by reference to which the contract has been made and that where the goods are supplied in the course of business they will be of satisfactory quality. In addition, there is an implied term that the person who hires the goods (the bailee) will enjoy quiet possession of the goods for the agreed period unless they are taken by the owner or another person with a right or charge over them which the bailee was told or knew about before the contract was made.

Quantum Meruit-when no price is agreed

This is a legal rule that is derived from previous cases rather than the supply of goods and services statute. It translates as "as much as he deserves" and means that if a price is not agreed before the work is completed, or if one party is prevented by the other, in breach of the contract, from completing the work he had contracted to perform then he may claim payment for the done on a quantum merit basis. A claim can also be made where the other party has voluntarily accepted partial performance.

The Cheque Rule

In a cheque issued to pay for goods or services is subsequently dishonoured, the recipient can base his claim on the cheque and does not have to prove the contract that led to its payment. This is because cheques, bills of exchange and promissory notes are regarded as independent contracts, separate from the contract for sale. Consequently there are only a few grounds on which a defendant can defend such a claim such of fraud, duress, total failure of consideration and possibly misrepresentation.

Unfair Contract terms Act, 1977

Contracts often include exclusion clauses, where one side attempts to limit its liability or the rights of the other party in the event of a breach of contract. The Unfair Contract Terms Act makes any clause excluding or limiting liability for death or personal injury void. Any exclusion clause that restricts or limits the terms implied by the Sale of Goods Act, where one party is dealing as a consumer, is void. This means that the exclusion has no effect. Any exclusion clause where one party is dealing on standard terms or one party is a business, will only be effective in so far as the person relying on it can prove that it is "reasonable" as defined by the Act which means that the terms "shall have been a fair and reasonable one to be included having regard to the circumstances which were, or contemplation of the parties when the contract was made". It is for the person alleging that a term or notice is reasonable to show that it is.

Personal Injuries- Tort

The Government is committed to increasing the Small Claims Court threshold from £1,000 to £5,000 for Road Traffic Accident claims – including whiplash – as part of its Civil Liability Act reforms. From April 2020, anyone injured in an RTA will not be able to instruct a lawyer to make a claim of £5,000 or less. For other personal injuries, the threshold will rise to £2,000 from £1,000.

For other personal injury claims are treated differently to other claims in that they are not automatically referred to small claims track if the damages claimed for "pain & suffering of amenity" exceed £1,000. This is because personal injury cases often raise difficult issues and the parties are more likely to need legal advice and representation the cost of which is not recoverable in small claims. Taking this £1,000 limit into account, £4,000 is the limit on other loss such as loss of earnings. You should consult the court staff about that point before beginning your case and in the case of a permanent or serious injury, you should take the advice of a Solicitor. Personal injuries can have been caused deliberately but in most cases the claimant seeks to prove that the defendant was negligent.

Four points must be proved to establish negligence:

- The defendant owed a duty of care, With regard to personal injuries, everyone should take reasonable care to avoid doing things or failing to do things, which they can reasonably foresee, would be likely to injure people who they ought reasonably to have foreseen as being so affected by their acts or omissions.
- The defendant acted in breach of his duty
- The breach caused the claimant's injury, and
- The injury was reasonably foreseeable, and not a "freak" accident"
- If the claimant was also negligent the court may find that he was guilty of contributory negligence and reduce the damages awarded to reflect the extent to which the claimant was responsible for causing his own injuries.

Breach of Statutory Duty-Tort

There are several areas in which statute imposes a duty on a public body such as a local authority or a private body such as an employer. For example, in the case of injury at work, the claimant could claim compensation on the grounds that the defendant acted in breach of the statutory duties imposed by the Health & Safety at Work legislation. These areas are complicated and research should be undertaken before taking legal action. However, in principle, a simple case could be suited to the small claims procedure.

Consumer Rights Act 2015 – Unsafe Goods

This Act allows action against a "producer" of goods, which are unsafe, and cause personal injury or loss of or damage to property provided the value of the claim is over £275, excluding interest. The term 'producer' includes the manufacturer, anyone who holds himself out as the producer by putting his name or trade mark on the product and the importer of the product into a Member State of the European Community from a place outside the EC in order to supply it to another in the course of his business. The Act does not apply to damage to the defective component comprised in it. Furthermore, there is no liability unless the product is a type of property ordinarily intended for private use, occupation or consumption and was intended by the claimant mainly for such purposes. A person who suffers damage to his business property must therefore sue on a contract or in negligence.

The Occupier's Liability Acts, 1957 & 1984 – Unsafe Premises

The 1957 Act governs the liability of an occupier in respect of personal injury or damage to property suffered by those who come lawfully onto his premises as visitors. An occupier is under a duty to take such care as in all circumstances of the case is reasonable, to see that the visitor will be reasonably safe in using the premises for the purpose for which he is invited or is permitted to be there. An occupier can discharge his duty by warning his visitor of the particular danger provided that the warning is sufficient to enable the visitor to be reasonably safe

The 1984 Act concerns the liability of an occupier with regard to people other than his visitors in respect of injuries suffered on the premises, due to the state of the premises, or things done or omitted to be done, on them. This includes trespassers and people exercising private rights of way but not those using public rights of way. The occupier owes such people a duty if he is aware of a danger or has reasonable grounds to believe one exists, if he knows or has reasonable grounds to believe that the non-visitor is in the vicinity of the danger concerned or that he may come into the vicinity and the risk is one against which in all the circumstances of the case he may reasonably be expected to offer the non-visitor some protection. An occupier may be able to discharge his duty by taking reasonable steps to warn people of the danger but whether the warning is adequate will depend on the circumstances.

The Rules mention specific claims such as a landlord's claim for disrepair and/or a tenant's claim for return of the deposit. The limit for such a claim to qualify for small claims track is £1,000. A claim for non-Payment of rent is an obvious example of a claim arising from housing.

Limitation Periods
The law imposes time limits, known as limitation periods within which you must commence your case. Time begins to run from the date of the breach of contract or the date of the actionable tort. Tort includes claims for negligence, which are not based on breach of contract, nuisance and occupiers liability. In personal injury cases it runs from the date when the injury was sustained or, if it is later from the date when the claimant first knew of their injuries. The court has the discretion to extend the time available in personal injury cases in certain circumstances.

The time limits are:

Contracts :6 years

Defective products (Consumer Protection Act 1987) 3 years

Personal injury: 3 years

If you are the defendant and the claimant's claim is out of time you will have a defence to the claim but it is important that you mention it on your defence.

Is it a Small Claims?

Claims for the possession of land cannot be dealt with under the small claims procedure and Employment disputes such as claims for unfair dismissal and sexual or racial discrimination are dealt with by Industrial Tribunals.

Allocation to Another Track

Where a claim is referred for the small claims track a district judge may order that it should not be treated as a small claim and there should be a trial in court instead, if:

- The case raises a difficult question of law or a complex question of fact or
- Fraud is alleged against any party or
- The parties agree that the case should be tried in court or
- It would not be reasonable for the case to proceed as a small claim having regard to its subject matter, the size of any counterclaim and the circumstances of the parties or the interests of any other person likely to be affected by the award.

The judge can do this on his own initiative or in response to an application by any party.

Research your claim –or risk failure

In every case, it is important to research the legal basis for your claim until you are sure that you are on solid foundations before a claim form is issued. Poor preparation means a reduced chance of success while good preparation will boost your confidence and help you see it through to the end. You can seek advice at Law Centres, Citizens Advice Centres, some libraries will stock legal books, and most university law libraries will admit a member of the public. You are free to instruct a Solicitor to prepare your statement of case if your claim is complicated.

****

]

Chapter 3.

Before Taking legal Action

Prevent claims Arising – Pre-emptive action

It is highly desirable to avoid litigation if at all possible and the best way to do this is to prevent claims arising. There is nothing to be gained by issuing proceedings prematurely when there is scope to settle the claim without involving the court. The parties are under a duty, imposed by the County Court Rules, to negotiate and to settle the dispute without involving the court if at all possible. This involves one or other forms of Alternative Dispute Resolution (ADR). At the end of this chapter we will also be discussing the process of mediation.

If you are a consumer and intend to employ someone to perform a service, obtain estimates beforehand outlining exactly what is to be done and how much it will cost. It is also wise to ask if the people you are doing business with belong to any professional or trade associations. Write and confirm all the details of the contract before the work begins. Disputes often result from oral contracts where neither party made a written record of what was agreed and understood by the parties at the time of the contract. Depending on the service you are buying, ensure that you have a written contract or that you use your standard terms of business in a sale or purchase. If you run a business, problems occur if credit is extended to the wrong customer or is allowed to extend beyond a suitable amount. Do not extend credit without first obtaining trade references or limit credit to a small figure. Insist on payment before further credit s extended and establish a track record with the customer before being too relaxed about extending credit. The best advice in the case of a "can't pay, won't pay" customer is to issue proceedings sooner rather than later because if the claim is defended you could be out of pocket for up to three months due to the slowness of the courts. If your business encounters serious problems in paying your creditors, negotiate terms of payment and discuss your situation openly and honestly. Such action at an early stage often avoids legal proceedings being taken against you. Always keep your bank manager informed and up to date with your business affairs and avoid giving him unexpected surprises.

Ensure that you keep all relevant documents, such as a receipt for a payment, the contract guarantees, delivery note or any letters written. Also keep a copy of any advertisement you relied on in entering into a contract. If you speak to anyone on the telephone, make a record of the person's name and of what was said.

Steps you should take before issuing a claim form

Before issuing a claim form, make a clear complaint and attempt to reach a compromise by contacting the defendant. If no compromise or settlement is achieved, before issuing a claim form, you should write to the defendant threatening legal action and stating the recompense you are demanding. It is important to be "proportionate" i.e. to write to the defendant with details of the claim before issuing proceedings. This is known as a "letter before action". It is important to keep a copy of this and of all correspondence to produce at the court hearing.

Is the defendant worth suing?

Before issuing a claim form to enforce a debt or payment of an invoice etc, consider whether the defendant is worth suing. If he or she is completely penniless, you may live a longer and more contented life if you decided not to take legal action.

Protocols and the letter of Claim

Before starting court proceedings, it is important to ensure that you have followed any pre-action protocols. Pre-action protocols are a series of steps each party must take before starting court proceedings. The intention of protocols is to encourage the early exchange of information which increases the chances of a settlement, or at least narrow the issues in dispute. It is in keeping with the over-riding objective where court action is regarded as the last resort.

A letter of claim should give sufficient information to identify the nature of the claim and give a reasonable opportunity to reply. The content will depend on whether the debtor is a business or an individual.

Letters of claim to Individual debtors:

The Protocol on Pre- Action Conduct is not intended to apply to debt claims where it is not disputed that the money is owed and where the claimant follows a statutory or other formal pre-action procedure. However, there is a requirement where the creditor is a business and the debtor is an individual, for the business to provide the debtor with information about sources of advice, before proceedings can be issued. Paragraph 7 of the Practice Direction deals with exchange of information before the start of proceedings and suggests that:

- A letter of claim is sent.
- The debtor should acknowledge the letter within 14 days and give a full response within a reasonable period of time, which for a straightforward undisputed debt is generally 14 days.
- Annex B to the Practice Directions sets out specific information that should be provided before starting proceedings in a debt claim by a claimant who is a business against a defendant who is an individual. Annex B makes provision for the information a claimant business should provide to the individual debtor and this is that the claimant should:

(1) Provide details of how the money can be paid (for example the method of payment and the address to which it can be sent):
(2) State that the defendant can contact the claimant to discuss possible repayment options, and provide the relevant contact details; and
(3) Inform the defendant that free independent advice and assistance can be obtained from organisations and then provide details of these organisations

The information about where an individual can obtain advice may be provided at any time between the claimant first intimating the possibility of court proceedings and the claimant's letter before claim. It may well be that your client has provided the information to the individual debtor before you are instructed to send the letter of claim. However, even if the client has already provided the information, it would prudent to avoid any doubt and reason for delay for the Letter of Claim to include the required information about seeking independent advice.

Where the defendant is unable to provide a full response within the time specified in the letter before claim because the defendant intends to seek debt advice, then the written acknowledgment should state:

(1) That the defendant is seeking advice;
(2) Who the defendant is seeking advice from; and
(3) When the defendant expects to have received that advice and be in a position to provide a full response.

A claimant should allow a reasonable period of time of up to 14 days for a defendant to obtain debt advice. However, the claimant need not allow the defendant time to seek debt advice if the claimant knows that the defendant has already received relevant debt advice and the defendant's circumstances have not significantly changed or the defendant has previously asked for time to seek debt advice but has not done so.

SAMPLE LETTERS BEFORE ACTION

See overleaf.

Dear Mrs. Gibson,

The washing machine I purchased from you on [date] is not of satisfactory quality or fit for the purpose for which it was sold. It has torn a number of garments of a total value of £600. I have already visited your shop and made a complaint but I have received no response.

I wish to return the faulty machine, have the purchase price refunded and for you to pay me the cost of replacing my clothes. If I do not receive a satisfactory reply within fourteen days I will begin legal proceedings against you in the County Court.

Yours sincerely,
J Smith

Dear Mrs Jones

Re: Our outstanding invoice number 1234567 for £766.34

I note that you have not yet paid our invoice issued on 13th August, a copy of which I enclose. I have written to you previously about this outstanding amount. Unless I receive payment immediately, or at least by the close of business on 30th September, then I will commence a claim against you in the county court.

Once I have commenced this claim I will be entitled to recover the court fee from you plus interest on the debt. I look forward to receiving the money from you.

We should inform you that free independent advice can be obtained from the organisations set out below

National Debtline: FREEPHONE 0808 808 4000

www.nationaldebtline.co.uk

Step Change FREEPHONE 0800 138 1111

www.stepchange.org

Citizens Advice: CHECK YOUR LOCAL DIRECTORY for
Numbers and addresses

If we do not receive a response from you within 14 days of the date of this letter, then our client will start court action against you to recover the outstanding sum.

Yours truly
J Smith

Small claims mediation service

This is for those who have started or received a claim for money through the small claims court and want to try free mediation to settle out of court.

About the service

The service is free and helps resolve cases relating to financial disputes, as an alternative to taking a claim through the formal court process. You work with a trained HM Courts and Tribunals Service mediator, who will help identify issues and work together to resolve them. You can access the service if:

- the claim in your case is up to £10,000
- you have already made or received a claim
- all the parties involved want to use the service

Types of cases that could benefit from mediation include:

- parking penalties
- online shopping
- building works
- unpaid invoices
- livestock or pet expenses

Mediation can be less expensive than going to court, where additional fees and expenses will apply. It can also be quicker than court, taking on average 2 to 3 weeks for a mediation appointment. The target wait for a court date is 30 weeks.

While mediation may help you avoid court, it will not delay your ongoing court process. You must continue to comply with all court directions. The session is confidential – if a solution is not found and your case goes to court, the court will not be told any of the mediation details.

How to access mediation
There are 2 ways that you may be invited for mediation. If you have received a:

- 'directions questionnaire', you should choose the option to be contacted about mediation.
- court order in the post recommending that your case is suitable for mediation, contact the small claims mediation service.

Both parties must contact the mediation service to use it. Contact the small claims mediation service
Telephone: 0300 123 4593
Monday to Friday, 9am to 5pm (except public holidays)
Email: scmreferrals@justice.gov.uk

Asking someone to represent you

If you want someone else to represent you at mediation, you must let the mediation service know so the person can be authorised. Your representative could be a trusted friend or relative, or a solicitor. This may be useful if you lack confidence in taking part in mediation because of a language barrier or other reason. Your representative must be fully aware of the facts and know how far you are willing to compromise.

How mediation works

Once both parties have requested mediation, you'll be given your telephone appointment date and time. The appointment will last up to 1 hour. At your appointment the mediator will:

- explain how the session will work and checking parties are prepared
- listen to each side separately – you won't talk directly to the other side
- help you reach an agreement if possible
- be impartial and will treat both parties with equal confidentiality
- not try to force you to find a settlement

Getting the most from mediation

To help your mediation:

- be open and flexible
- be willing to work with the mediator to find a resolution
- be clear with what you want to say
- be able to answer any questions
- have a quiet, private space where you won't be disturbed
- be available at the start of the session and throughout

What happens next

If mediation succeeds You will receive a legally binding settlement agreement. This will explain what actions each party must take next.

This could be:
- full payment of the claim
- a reduced payment
- a payment in instalments
- a charitable donation in place of the claim payment
- an exchange of product or service
- credit or vouchers
- completion of a contract

You can apply to the court to enforce the agreement if it is broken by the other party.

If mediation is unsuccessful

If you don't reach an agreement in mediation, or you are unable to settle with the other party after mediation, the case will continue to the court hearing

If the claim is for more than £50.000 then the fees should be agreed in advance with the mediator.

.****

Chapter 4.

An Overview of Procedure

Part 7 governs the issue of the claim form. If a defence is not filed, judgement is entered for the claimant because the defendant is in default of the obligation to file a defence. If a defence is filed, the claim is in appropriate circumstances allocated to the small claims track and proceeds under the provisions of Part 27.

The procedure for small claims is informal. The district judge hears the case in a private room although the hearing is now open to the public if they wish to attend, (in practice this is seldom the case). You can claim fixed costs, your own personal costs, witness expenses and in certain cases expert fees for reports (only if the judge gives permission to use an expert witness). Solicitors' fees are not awarded to the successful party. You should check entitlement at the time of going to court as they are subject to change. At the time of writing legal aid budgets are being drastically cut. This is to encourage members of the public to conduct their own case. The small claims procedure is designed for lawyer-free self-representation.

In certain cases, expenses for travel and overnight accommodation may be claimed. The Court provides standard forms for completion by the opponents throughout a case with the intention that for simple matters, you could present your own case. The same forms are available from the Lord Chancellor's homepage.

Types of Small Claim

Your claim may be for a fixed amount or for an amount to be assessed. In the latter case, liability for the claim is treated separately from assessment of the amount of the claim. In such a case, you would write on the claim form e.g. "not more than £3,000" when the claim is for between £1,000 and £3,000. If a defence is not filed or if such a claim is admitted, you would obtain judgement with damages to be assessed by the district judge at a "disposal hearing". In most cases, you will know the amount of your claim.

Special Features of Part 7 Procedures

- The claimant is entitled to Judgement in default of the defendant filing the Acknowledgement of service and/or the defence, or
- Judgement on liability with damages to be assessed at a disposal hearing

Special features of the Small Claims Track

- Complicated rules do not apply
- The hearing is informal and not in open court although the public can attend. If defended the case is heard in the defendant's home court. The rules for this are set out in Part 7 which deals with money claims on line.

Completing and Issuing a Claim Form

If you want to make a county court money claim you must send the claim form to the "County Court Money Claims Centre" (CCMCC) or if you don't want to use the CCMC, then you will have to use Money Claims On-Line (see below). This change was part of improvements to the administration of civil business.

Cases will be issued at the CCMCC and where they become defended and ready to be allocated to a track, they will be transferred to an appropriate county court. Claim Forms can be posted to the CCMC at:

Salford Business Centre
PO Box 527
Salford
M5 0BY

Any enquiries on cases proceeding at the CCMCC should be made to the following:

For email enquiries: ccmcccustomerenquiries@hmcts.gov.uk
For e-filing enquiries: ccmcc-filing@hmcts.gov.uk
For telephone enquiries: 0300 1231372

It is important to complete the claim form as accurately as you can. The Claim Form (NI) is shown at the end of this book in Appendix B. Once the claim form has been served on the defendant, permission is needed from the defendant to amend it and if that is not forthcoming then you would have to apply to the court. So ensure you have entered the details correctly and that you have named the defendant correctly. If the defendant is a business then it is important to have the correct legal entity of the organisation. Is the business an incorporated company? If it is, then there should be the word "LTD" or "Limited" after its name. A limited company should have the registered company number on its headed paper and so you can use this number to check the full company name and registered office by visiting Companies House website. It is advisable to state the registered office of a company as the address where the court should send the claim. This should remove any doubts of service. You can of course always send a copy of the claim to the trading address after the court has sent it to the registered office. On the claim form there must be a statement of value. The statement of value should be inserted below the word "Value" on the front page of the claim form. The form of wording should be: "Value: £X plus accrued interest and fixed costs.

In deciding which level of court fee the claim comes within, the court takes into account the interest claimed to the date of the claim.

In a personal injury claim, for example, where you would be claiming general damages for pain and suffering, statement of value would be worded, for example, as " the claimant expects to recover between £5,000 and £15,000".

The particulars of claim must be verified by a statement of truth. The person signing a statement of truth can be guilty of contempt of court if they know that the facts contained within the document are untrue. A solicitor can sign the statement of truth in his own name but states that: "The Claimant believes......". A solicitor should check the contents of the particulars of claim with his client before he signs it on their behalf. If the statement of truth is being signed by an officer of a company, that person must be at a senior level, such as a manager or director.

On the front page of the claim form, there are boxes where you enter the amount of the claim. There is a box for fixed solicitors' costs as allowed by the court rules. These fixed costs can only be claimed if you have a solicitor acting for you.

There is a court fee to issue a court claim. The level of fee depends on the amount claimed. The latest court fees can be obtained from the Court Service website. If a case is defended and progresses to a hearing then there will be further fees to pay. The following shows the further fees payable depending on the track the case is allocated to:

Small Claims Track	Allocation Fee (if over £1,500)	Hearing Fee	
Fast Track	Allocation Fee	Listing Fee	Hearing Fee
Multi Track	Allocation Fee	Listing Fee	Hearing Fee

The current policy of the Ministry of Justice is to make county courts self-financing which has caused a steady increase in court fees. If you are an individual and are either on a qualifying state benefit or your disposable income is below a certain level, you may be able to obtain a full or part fee remission, which means that you will not have to pay all or part of the required court fee. To claim for a "fee remission", you will have to complete the relevant application form and supply up to date documentary evidence regarding your finances. Fee remissions are not available for business. If a claim is issued through the Claim Production Centre, then the court fee is discounted. The Claim Production Centre is designed for those issuing a large number of debt actions.

Freezing Orders

A creditor can prevent a debtor from moving assets out of reach by applying for a freezing order. A freezing order is an injunction which prevents a party from removing assets out of the country or from dealing with the assets. Application for a freezing injunction are usually made to the High Court, but there are exceptions where an order can be granted by a county court such as where it is sought to aid execution after judgment. If you are considering applying for a freezing order, it is strongly recommended that you seek the assistance of a solicitor.

Making a Claim Online

Those with access to the internet can start a claim for money online. To start the claim, you need to visit the Court Service website: www.moneyclaim.gov.uk/web/mcol/welcome

With Money Claims Online, the claim has to be for a fixed amount that is less than £100,000. You have to pay for the court fees by credit or debit card. Users of this system cannot obtain an exemption from court fees.

Response Pack

The court will then serve (i.e. post) the claim form on the defendant with a "RESPONSE Pack" containing four forms, a Form of Acknowledgement, a Form of Admission (N9A), a form for filing a Defence (N9B) and a form for filing a Counterclaim (N9B)

Admitted or Part Admitted Claims: Part 14

The DEFENDANT may either

- Admit/Part admit the claim with an offer to pay immediately. The court will enter judgement.
- Admit/Part admit the claim with an offer to pay in instalments.
- If the claim is part admitted, a defence should be filed to show why part of the claim is not admitted
- If the claim is for an unspecified amount i.e. an amount to be assessed, the defendant can admit the claim and make an offer.

The CLAIMANT may then

- File an application for judgement of the admitted claim
- Accept or reject an offer of instalments on an admitted claim. If you reject the instalments offered, the court clerk will assess the defendant's statement of means and make an order for instalments. If you are dissatisfied with the clerk's decision, you may apply to the district judge for a determination.
- Reject a part admission; in which case the claim proceeds as if defended. And the defendant should file a defence.
- In the case of an admitted claim with the "amount to be assessed", you should apply for judgement to be entered for liability. The court will schedule a "disposal hearing"

to determine the amount of the claim or damages payable. If an offer is made in respect of a claim for an unspecified sum, the offer may be either accepted or rejected. If it is rejected, the court will proceed to a "disposal hearing" for damages to be assessed

Refuted Claims

The defendant may as an alternative to admitting the claim:

- File the acknowledgement requesting 28 days to file the defence; or
- File a defence within 14 days; and/or
- File a counterclaim against the claimant; and/or
- Issue a Part 20 Notice against a non-party or a contribution notice against a co-defendant

Judgement in Default

If the defendant does not file a defence within 14 days of the date of service of the claim (or 28 days from filing the acknowledgement of service), the court will at the request of the claimant order judgement in the claimant's favour without a hearing. This is judgement "in default" of the defendant filing a defence. The claimant should file a request for a default judgement after the time period has lapsed. If the amount of the claim is not specified on the claim form, then as indicated above, you should file the request and the court will order judgement for the claimant with damages to be assessed at a disposal hearing.

Defence

The defence is a statement of case and Part 16 requires that it states (a) which allegations in the particulars of claim are denied

(b) which are not admitted or denied i.e. that the claimant must prove, and (c) which allegations are admitted. If an allegation is denied, the defendant must (a) state his reason for denying it and (b) if he intends to put forward a different version of events, state his own version. In the case of a defendant who files a Defence, the court will serve a copy on the claimant and the case will be transferred to the defendant's local or "home" court, which will process the claim along the small claims track. If you expect the defendant to file a defence, you will save time if you issue your claim form in his local County Court.

Counterclaim : Part 20

The defendant may make a counterclaim

- This will be heard with the claim. A court fee will be payable (see chapter 15)
- If the counterclaim is above the small claims limit of £10,000 the district judge may allocate the claim to a different track.

The defendant's counterclaim is a claim made by the defendant against the claimant, which may be less than his claim, so his claim is reduced, or it may be greater. A counterclaim is a separate action and an alternative to the defendant issuing his own claim form. Both claims are therefore managed in one action or set of proceedings. The defendant is in the same position as the claimant when making a counterclaim. The rules for the content of the counterclaim are the same as for any claim. The claimant must file a defence to the counterclaim to avoid judgement-in-default on the counterclaim. In this respect, the claimant is for the purposes of the counterclaim in the same position as a defendant and the rules governing the content of the defence apply. Counterclaims are dealt with under Part 20.

This Part also deals with claims by one defendant against another and circumstances in which a defendant wishes to issue proceedings against a non-party. If you as the defendant to a claim, or a defendant to a counterclaim, consider either to be applicable you should instruct a Solicitor.

Allocation to a Track: Allocation Questionnaire Form

If the defendant files a defence or counterclaim, the Court will:

- Post a form called an "Allocation Questionnaire" (N205A) TO THE PARTIES. This form records the details of the claim, the case number and date of service. The case number is now the reference point for your case and no steps can be taken without quoting it
- Both parties must complete and file the Allocation Questionnaire. The claimant must pay a fee when filing this form.

Directions Issued by the Court

After the Allocation Questionnaire is received, or in default of filing the Allocation Questionnaire, the court will allocate the claim to the small claims track and issue directions. These are the courts instructions as to how the case should proceed. District judges have wide powers to issue directions but for small claims PD27 provides standards form directions depending on the category of claim. The parties may apply for directions using form N244.

Enforcement Proceedings

If the defendant does not comply with a court order or judgement, you must take enforcement proceedings to enforce the judgement.

Chapter 5.

More on Completing the Claim Form

___

The Claim Form (N1) (see Appendix 1)

Although we touch on the completion of the claim form 9 in the previous chapter, it is necessary to touch on this aspect of making a small claim in more depth as it is important to get this right the first time round. It is best to have the claim form in front of you when reading this chapter.

The claim form has space for names of the parties, brief details of the claim, the value (if a value statement is required), a box for the defendant's address, and box for amount claimed, court fee, solicitors costs (i.e. fixed costs are recoverable for a Solicitor to prepare the form), total amount and issue date. The back of the form is for Particulars of Claim, the statement of truth and claimants address.

The claim form requires the claimant's full name. If the claimant is a company give the address of the registered office. If it is a firm write "a firm " after the name, If you use a trade name write your name and then " trade as " followed by your business name. Think carefully about whether you are the correct person in bringing the action. For example, if your spouse or friend gave you a present that turns out to be faulty, and you want a refund of the purchase price, then the person who actually bought the goods should be the claimant.

Identify the defendant

Wrongly identifying the defendant is one of the most common errors in small claims cases. If the incorrect defendant is sued, the proceedings will be delayed.

Claims against shops

Every business is obliged to display a prominent notice at its premises which gives the names and addresses of the owners of the business (s.4 of the Business Names Act 1985). If the name of the owner of the business is not known, then the defendant should be shown as (Name of Business) followed by the words "a trading name".

If the owner of the business can be identified, for example from the Business Names Act Sign in the shop, then the defendant should be shown as "(name of owner)" followed by words "trading as (name of shop)".

Claims against firms

If details of the owners of the business cannot be found, then proceedings can be issued in the trading name of the business. The position then is the same as for claims against shops, as above.

Limited companies

If the firm's notepaper, website or the notice displayed at the shop reveals that the prospective defendant is a limited company then that is the name which should be used on the claim form. Any individual, director or employee should not be named as the defendant.

Directors of limited companies

The general rule is that where there is a claim against a limited company then it is the company and not the directors or managers who are sued.

Claims against partnerships

Partners can be sued either in the trading names of the partnership, or in the individual names of the partners themselves.

Principals and agents

This is a difficult area and requires careful thought before issuing proceedings. However, the following basic legal principles should be borne in mind:

- An agent does not deal on his or her own behalf but only on behalf of the principal
- Any court action must be against the principal and not against the agent.

It is sometimes difficult to tell who is the principal and who is the agent. This must be resolved at the outset before taking legal action.

Companies in liquidation

Proceedings should not be issued against companies in liquidation and any claim must be referred to the liquidator-details of the liquidators will be found at companies house.

Claims against bankrupts

Proceedings cannot be issued against a bankrupt for any debt or claim which arose before the date of bankruptcy except with the permission of the court. Most claims against bankrupts should be referred to the Trustee in bankruptcy. If the claim or debt arose after the date of bankruptcy then the bankrupt can be sued. However, if the claim involves the bankrupt obtaining credit after the date of the bankruptcy then an offence may have been committed and the Trustee in bankruptcy should be notified immediately. The box in the left hand corner is for the defendant's address and the claimant's address is inserted in the box in the same position on the reverse side of the claim form. If the defendant is a company the address of its registered office will be on its headed notepaper, or you can find it out by telephoning Companies House in Cardiff on 0303 1234 500.

Category of Claim

A brief description of what type of claim you are making is required in the next space. This means stating what the claim consists of, for example breach of contract, dishonoured cheque, non-payment of invoice or bad workmanship.

Statement of Case: Part16

The particulars or details of your claim must be set out in the largest box on the reverse side of the form, or on a separate piece of paper. The requirements of Part 16/PD16 are set out in chapter 5. It is important to use numbered paragraphs and to set out each point relevant to your case.

For example in a claim for breach of contract, you should state the following:

- That a contract was entered into with the defendant
- When it was made, was it written or oral, and if oral, the way in which it may be evidenced e.g. by reference to letters and documents
- The relevant terms of the contract including implied terms. For example terms implied by the Sale of Goods Act
- That you have performed all or part of your side of the contract or why you have not done so
- That the contract has been breached and give details of what the defendant has done or failed to do that puts him in breach
- What damages you have suffered as the result of the defendant's breach of the contract and the term or provision that the defendant has not complied with.
- And lastly, you must state what you claim; for example payment of an invoice (state the amount) and interest at the contractual or statutory rate.

If your claim is in tort such as personal injury rather than contract, for example you are alleging that the defendant was negligent, then you must state the following:

- Who the parties are (if relevant)
- Describe the accident or event which is the basis of your complaint and say when it took place
- That the accident or act you are complaining about was caused by the defendant's negligence or breach of duty and give details
- That you suffered damage as a result of the facts alleged and give details of all the damage

- And lastly, state what you are claiming by either stating the amount claimed, or that you would like damages to be assessed, and claim interest.
- Any claim for personal injury must comply with the Pre-Action Protocol.

You should then sign the statement of truth and file two copies at the court. Keep a copy for your records.

Practice Direction 16

PD 16 identifies specific matters that must be addressed in the particulars of claim for personal injury, fatal accident claims, claims for recovery of land, and hire purchase claims. In particular, if relevant, the written contract or relevant conditions of sale should be attached to the claim form. Where the claim is based on an oral contract, the particulars of claim should state the contractual words used, who said these words, where and when they were said. If the contract is to be proved by conduct or a course of dealing, the particulars must state the conduct or acts relied upon and by whom, when and where the acts constituting the conduct were done.

Duty to Mitigate

The claimant is under a positive duty to take steps to minimise or reduce the loss suffered as a result of the defendants' breach of contract or breach of duty. The claim should be for the loss suffered after mitigation.

Statement of Truth

Each statement of case and witness statement must be endorsed with a signed Statement of Truth. A false statement which is verified by a statement of truth is a contempt of court and penalties for contempt would apply if the judge took the matter further. When issuing online, the claimant is invited to confirm the statement of truth by adding their name; this fulfils the requirement to sign the statement of truth.

Human rights

You must complete the tick box about the human rights element, the ticking (or ignoring) of the box has no effect at all on the claim even if the claim includes any issue under the Human Rights Act 1998. The tick box has been introduced merely to help the court service to keep tabs on the issue of such claims.

Decide if the claim is specified or unspecified

A claim which is specified, for example a debt claim, is for a fixed amount of money. All claims for money are specified. A claim is unspecified if the amount involved is not precisely known at the outset (for example damages for distress). Any claim which is left to the court to decide is unspecified. This is relevant to a number of practical matters, namely:

- The choice of issue court and transfer between courts if the defendant is an individual
- Checking that the value is within the small claims limit
- Calculating the court fee
- Entering judgement in full.

Claim for Interest

Claiming interest in the small claims court You are entitled to ask for Interest on the amount you are claiming, this is currently 8%

per year. If you want to claim interest you must put on your claim that you want your opponent to pay interest.

What to do next

Take the two copies of the complete claim form to the court, along with a copy for each defendant, and pay the issue fee. Remember to keep a copy for yourself. The court may ask for copies. The court will stamp the claim from and post it to the defendant with forms of admission, defence and counterclaim, explained in the next chapter.

The defendant must reply to your claim form within 14 days from the date of service printed on the Allocation Questionnaire. If the defendant files a defence, the court will post a copy to you. A form of Admission is returned direct to the claimant.

****

Chapter 6.

The Defendant-Responding to the Claim Form

This chapter examines the position of a defendant. The court serves the claim form on the defendant with the Response Pack containing forms for Admission, Defence and Counterclaim. The claimant is also a defendant when a counterclaim has been filed. The counterclaim is equivalent to a claim and the claimant must file a defence to the counterclaim or judgement in default would be available to the defendant/claimant. The effect of filing a defence is that the court will post Allocation Questionnaire forms to both parties. When the Allocation Questionnaires are returned, the claim will be allocated to the small claims track, directions will be issued, and a hearing will be arranged.

Judgement in Default of a Defence

If a judgement debt is not paid, a record is maintained on the Register of County Court Judgements for six years. This register is open to credit reference agencies. If judgement in default is entered against you, then you must either:

- Apply for it to be set aside, or
- Pay the sum demanded, and/or
- Apply to pay by instalments

Admit, Defend and/or Counterclaim

If you do not admit the claim or file a defence, and/or counterclaim, the court will then enter "judgement-in –default" against you at the request of the claimant. This means that the court will order you to either:

- Pay the sum demanded, or
- In the case of an unspecified sum, judgement will be entered against you with damages to be assessed at a disposal hearing.

Form of Admission (N9A-N9C)

The effect of an admission is that the claimant will be entitled to judgement in respect of the amount you admit. The issue then is the method of payment and whether the claimant or the court will permit payment by instalments. It is possible just to admit part of the claim if you believe that the claimant is not entitled to the whole amount but in such a case, you must use the forms of defence and/or counterclaim to deny that you owe the balance of the claim. If an admission is filed but the claimant does not accept your offer to pay by instalments, the court staff will set an amount with reference to the information you supply. If you object to the level of instalments ordered by court staff, you are entitled to make an application for the district judge to assess the level of instalments.

The Form of Defence/Counterclaim (N9B-N9D)

If you deny that the claimant's claim is valid you must file a defence. However you can only file a defence if you have a reason for disputing the claimant's claim and not just a reluctance to pay him. Examples are that work done was faulty, the wrong goods were supplied and that the debt is really owed to another person. You should also file a defence if you admit part of the claim and the claimant will not accept your offer of part payment in full settlement. You must say why you do not owe the full amount.

Preparing the Defence

The defence must answer every claim made in the statement of case and make allegations on behalf of the defendant. In essence, each claim must be admitted or denied. Use numbered paragraphs if at all possible, unless the defence is simple. Look very careful at the claimant's claim. Go through the statement of case methodically and try to respond to every allegation by denying it, admitting it or saying that you do not know. If you deny something then the claimant must prove the allegation. If you admit something it means that the claimant does not have to prove that particular point and the court will take it as accepted. It is important to also put forward your side of the story summarising what really happened and why it means you are not liable to the claimant as he claims. However, remember that if you are making a claim of your own against the claimant, then the allegations that relate to this should be made in the counterclaim and not in the defence.

As well as putting forward an alternative version or interpretation of events you can also take issue with the amount of damage the claimant claims to have suffered. For example, you might say that goods, which were damaged, are not as valuable as the claimant claims or his injury was not as serious as the claimant suggests.

You are also entitled to expect a claimant to mitigate these losses. This means that the claimant must take all reasonable steps to minimise the loss suffered even if the defendant was at fault. The claimant is not entitled to recover damages that the defendant can prove resulted from a failure to mitigate. If you are unsuccessful in your defence, the court will order you to pay the full amount the claimant is seeking.

The Form of Counterclaim- Part 20

If you wish to make a claim against the claimant, you may file a counterclaim. This is equivalent to issuing your own claim form against the claimant. The counterclaim is a separate action that will be considered with the original claim. As with a claimant's original claim, you must request either a fixed amount or damages to be assessed. If the counterclaim is in excess of the small claims limit this does not prevent the case being automatically referred to small claims track but it is one of the factors a district judge can take into account when considering whether the case should be allocated to the small claims track. A court fee will be payable if the counterclaim exceeds the claim against you. The counterclaim should be particularised using numbered paragraphs that state clearly what you claim, why the claimant is liable and what compensation you require. The claimant should file a defence to your counterclaim or you will be entitled to judgement in default.

Setting Aside a Default Judgement

If a Default Judgement is made against you when you have a "real prospect of successfully defending the claim", the court has discretion to set aside the default judgement. You may apply to the Court for the judgement to be set aside by using form N244.

Your application must be supported by evidence i.e. a witness statement verified by a statement of truth. You must give reasons for failure to file a defence and convince the judge that your defence is genuine. The court must have regard to whether the application was made promptly, and conditions may be imposed on allowing you to defend e.g. that a defence is filed within 14 days. Delay in making the application after judgement in default is received could be fatal to its success. In practice, the proposed defence should be attached to the witness statement filed in support of the application, or at the very least, the witness statement should set out what defence is available to the defendant.

Transfer to the Defendant's "home court"

The application to set aside the claim will be heard at the defendant's local court unless the claimant can give good reasons why it should not be transferred.

Claims against Others- Part 20

A defendant who holds a third party entirely or partly responsible for the claimant's loss is entitled to join the third party in the action by issuing a Part 20 Notice. Leave of the court is required to issue the Notice if the defence has been filed. An example of where you might want to join a third party is if the claimant brings an action seeking compensation for damage to his car caused by you driving into the back of it. But you only hit the claimant's vehicle because your car was shunted forward as result of being hit by third party's car. In such circumstances you would want the third party to be joined in the action as he is the person who is really responsible for the damage.

Chapter 7.

Settling the Dispute Before Trial

It may be worth your while to try and reach a compromise with your opponent and to settle the case without a small claims track hearing. This is because all litigation contains some element of risk. However much you believe in your own case there is almost always a chance that the district judge's decision could go against you. By reaching a settlement you save yourself the risk of losing completely in return for conceding something to your opponent. You also save yourself the time and trouble involved in arguing the merits of the case in front of the district judge. Think carefully about the strengths and weaknesses of your case, and then decide what you would be prepared to accept. It is important to be realistic. Any counterclaim should be settled at the same time.

How to Negotiate a Settlement

If you want to reach a settlement you can write to your opponent and make them an offer. Letters concerning settlements are usually headed "without prejudice". The practical effect of heading your letter "without prejudice" is that if your opponent refuses your offer or ignores it, then the letter and its contents cannot be used as evidence against you. This means you can make admissions in "without prejudice" correspondence and "horse trade" in the knowledge that your concessions will not count against you. The letter before action should not be without prejudice and it should make a claim at the highest level you consider your claim is worth. If the offer is accepted after without prejudice correspondence, it should be agreed in open correspondence to become a binding agreement to settle action.

You could also write to your opponent and ask if he would be prepared to discuss the case on the telephone or arrange a meeting in the hope that you can negotiate a settlement. If you do not know your opponent well, exercise caution if the dispute is heated.

When entering into negotiations it is important to be prepared. It is a good idea to write down three figures in advance. Firstly, an opening offer or request which might be slightly more than you expect to receive or less than you expect to pay, secondly the figure you would be happy to accept or to pay and thirdly your bottom line which is the minimum you would accept or the maximum you would pay your opponent. It is particularly important to decide on the final figure and keep it in mind so that an aggressive opponent cannot push you into an unfavourable settlement.

When to Negotiate

You are free to negotiate at any time, from before the start of legal proceedings until the district judge makes his judgement. In small claims the disclosure of evidence normally takes place only one or two weeks before the date set for small claims track. If you feel that seeing your opponent's documents and expert's reports is likely to effect your view of the strength or weakness of their case it may be worth waiting until you receive copies before reaching any agreement.

When to Accept an Offer

If your opponent makes you an offer of settlement consider what his motives may be. If it is very low it could be that he has misjudged the strength of his own case but alternatively he may have spotted a genuine weakness in your case that you have not noticed. You are free to ask him why he thinks that amount is reasonable. If the offer is high you will naturally want to come to a decision quickly in case it is withdrawn but you should not necessarily accept it immediately. There may be a weakness in his case you do not yet know about or yours might be stronger than you think. If a relatively large sum is involved it might be worth taking advice on whether or not to accept it.

Consent Orders

The court will normally approve a settlement that both sides accept. This is achieved by a consent order. A formal form of consent may be signed and filed with the Court any time before the hearing.

The parties are under a general duty to attempt a negotiated settlement and to inform the court if agreement is achieved in advance of the hearing. The court would obviously prefer to save time and deal with the consent order by post. Both sides should write to the court outlining their agreement; or for one party to set out the agreed compromise and the other to sign at the foot of the letter. The judge must approve a consent order before or at the hearing. At the hearing, if a compromise were agreed, the judge would record the agreement and the court draws up a consent order or judgement.

Withdrawing the Claim Form

If a settlement has been agreed, the claimant may file a Notice of Discontinuance (Form N297) and a certificate saying that the defendant has been informed of withdrawal of the claim form. The case would be ended without a court order.

This option may be suitable if the claimant simply abandons the case altogether, or if the defendant pays an agreed sum in one payment. If instalments are agreed, the claimant is better off with a court order that is capable of enforcement. A consent order would be preferable to a discontinuance.

****

Chapter 8.

Preparing For The Hearing

Preliminary Appointments
The court controls what steps should be taken before the hearing by issuing "directions". The usual directions for a small claims track case are listed in Practice Direction 27. Either party can make an application to the court on form N244 for a preliminary appointment at which the party may request additional directions. You may wish to apply for additional directions if the standard directions do not cover all the points. Your main concern will be directions concerning evidence, and disclosure of evidence such as documents, or for permission to produce photographs.

It is not usually necessary in small claims proceedings to require non-standard directions. The other party may oppose your application or not attend the hearing. If at all possible, try and agree the directions with your opponent then both parties can write to the court asking for the same direction. In nearly all cases, the court will grant any directions which both parties request.

A preliminary appointment is informal and takes place in a private room with a district judge and the litigants present. Remember, a preliminary appointment is not the small claims track. Beyond establishing whether or not you have an arguable claim or defence the judge will not consider the merits of the case at this stage so you do not need to take along witnesses or to be fully prepared to argue your case at this point.

Applications Generally-Form 244

An application used to require a hearing. Under the new rules, form 244 allows the applicant to indicate that he wishes the judge to deal with the application without a hearing. If the subject matter of the application is contentious or disputed, it is safer to request a hearing. Preliminary applications attract a court fee of £50. All applications must be supported by evidence i.e. a witness statement.

Failure to Attend a Preliminary Appointment

The district judge may order a preliminary appointment. If the claimant fails to attend despite the judge's order, the judge will probably strike the case out. If the defendant does not attend, the judge could either issue directions, strike out the defence, or if the admission is filed, allow the claimant to prove the level of loss suffered.

Trial Date & Time Estimates

If it has not done so already the court will set a date for the small claims track. If you cannot attend on the date set inform the court immediately. The judge who issues the directions will give a time estimate of how long he expects the case to last. If the time estimate is too short, write to the court and/or telephone the listings clerk because otherwise the judge may not have time to hear your case in full and you will have to go back another date.

Another appointment is unlikely to be immediately available so this will mean you have to wait longer to get the case resolved. Either the claimant or the defendant can ask for more time. Allow plenty of time for your witnesses to give their evidence and to be questioned by your opponent.

Complying with Directions

It is essential that you comply with the district judge's directions concerning what should be done and exchanged before the trial. Failure to exchange documentary evidence and expert reports may mean that you cannot use such evidence during the small claims track hearing and this could seriously harm your prospects of success.

Your Own Preparations for the Small Claims Track

Although small claims hearings are informal, many people feel apprehensive at the prospect of presenting their case to the district judge. The better you prepare before the hearing the more confident you will be when you attend the small claims track. Remember that you are a witness in your own case and that the issues are defined in your statement of case and the defence. In general, there is a conflict in the evidence and the district judge will be deciding whose evidence he finds most credible. The strict procedure is that the claimant makes a case and the defendant then presents a defence, as follows:

- The claimant. You will have to be prepared to introduce the case to the district judge by telling him what it is about, what happened, why the defendant was at fault and what is at issue or in dispute .It is a good idea to write a list of important points in the order you want to mention them so that you do not forget things or repeat yourself. Look back at your particulars of claim and the defence to make sure you have not overlooked anything. If you can, find an obliging friend, practice explaining your case and ask them if what you say is clear and easy to follow.

- The defendant. You will have to respond to the claimant's claims or rebut his allegations. However, you will know in advance what claims have been made, so you will be able to predict much of what the claimant will say. Look at the particulars of claim and the documents you receive from the claimant such as expert's reports. Make your own note of the key allegations being made against you and then be prepared to outline your defence to the district judge rebutting each of these allegations. Make a list of the points you intend to make in order. You may benefit from practice in explaining your defence to a friend or relative.

- Preparing to deal with witnesses. Once you have outlined your claim or defence you will have the opportunity to call witnesses to give evidence. Before the small claims track, reflect on why you are calling each witness and what you hope they will say that will strengthen your case or weaken your opponents. Prepare a few questions with which you could prompt them to discuss the relevant matter without actually giving the court the evidence yourself. For example: "What did you see after the red car came around the corner of Smith Street?" is preferable to "The defendant drove around the corner of Smith Street too fast, swerved all over the road and then negligently drove over my bicycle, didn't he ?"

- The district judge will have already heard your account of events; he now wants to hear from the witness. You may undermine the strength of his evidence if you, in effect, tell him what to say. Preparing questions in advance will help you to resist the natural temptation to try and give the witness's evidence for him. You will also get an opportunity to question your opponent's witnesses, this is known as cross-examination. When doing this the recommendation about not giving evidence for them does not apply, in that you can make a statement of fact such as "the defendant was going too fast wasn't he?" or "the claimant had left his bicycle in the middle of the road hadn't he?" and ask them for a yes or no answer.

- Try to think in advance of anything, which weakens or discredits their evidence. For example that they could not have had a very good view of the accident, they are in business with your opponent, or their memory of events is imperfect on one point so should not be relied on in relation to another question.

- In general when you are preparing for the hearing it is a good idea to try and step back from the case. This is difficult as you will naturally feel strongly about your claim or defence but if you can try and see it from an impartial viewpoint and then try and think from your opponent's perspective you may get a clearer appreciation of the strengths and weaknesses of your case and be better able to predict what will be raised at the small claims track.

- In preparation for the hearing have plenty of copies of the documents with you because you may have to supply them to the district judge or your opponent and photocopying at court costs £1 for every sheet.

It could also be worth your while trying to reach agreement with your opponent before the small claims track hearing.

Witness statements

The most basic standard directions (Form A attached to Practice Direction 27) do not require witness statements to be prepared. This simply requires that all documents be exchanged with copies filed in court and the originals to be brought to the hearing. It is open to you, nevertheless, to prepare and file a witness statement voluntarily. This practice would give the court advanced notice of your case beyond the statement of case, and the documents and/or photographs you rely on can be attached to the witness statement and referred to.

Your evidence should be written and any other witnesses should file witness statements with copies served on the defendant. This will help you present your case at the hearing if you can refer to your statement when issues arise.

Evidence

Our legal system is in principle adversarial and not inquisitorial. This means that both parties to a dispute must present a case to a judge who acts as an impartial observer. The small claims procedure is an exception to this rule in that the judge will be more involved. He will ask questions and try and find out what he needs to know. Nevertheless it is the responsibility of the parties to supply the evidence for the judge to consider.

Types of Evidence

Evidence is factual information that can be presented to the court to enable the judge to decide on the probability of a claim that has been made being correct or true. In all cases, the claimant and the defendant are witnesses in their own case. The claims made in particulars of claim or in a defence or any other statement of case must be proven with evidence. Evidence can take a number of different forms:

Oral Evidence. Both the claimant and the defendant will be able to give evidence by speaking to the district judge, giving their account of events and presenting their arguments. They can also call witnesses to attend court and give oral evidence about any relevant fact of which they have knowledge. If a witness is unwilling to attend the hearing, you are entitled to compel their attendance by issuing a witness form (Form N20). This must be done at least seven days before the hearing, and it will mean that you have to pay the witnesses' expenses and cost of their travel to and from the court. Court staff will tell you how much this is. If you are successful and win the case you should be able to recover the cost of the witnesses travelling and overnight expenses reasonably incurred and £50 for their loss of earnings from your opponent. However, check current expenses as they are subject to change.

.Witness Statements. In general, the oral evidence should be supported by witness statements, filed in court and served on the other party. This is not one of the standard directions and therefore not a strict requirement but it is a good tactic to prepare and serve witness statements regardless of the directions made by the court. Witnesses who are unable to attend the hearing can give their evidence in writing. They should give their full name and address and sign and date their statement. Such evidence can be very useful but, depending on the circumstances, it is likely to carry less weight than direct oral testimony because the other party and the judge do not have the opportunity to question the witness, and because seeing someone give their evidence would help the district judge to decide how credible he finds that witness. On the other hand, if you get your witness to make a statement prior to the hearing and ask your opponent if they will accept that the evidence contained in the statement is correct you may be able to save the cost and trouble of bringing the witness to court. Witness statements are also useful where you have a number of witnesses who are going to say the same thing. You can ask one of them to attend the hearing and request that the others make statements. Photocopies of witness statements should be given to the other party prior to the hearing in accordance with the court's directions.

Photographs & Documentary Evidence. This includes things like contracts, letters, a returned cheque, estimates, delivery notes, receipts, diary entries, guarantees and photographs. Judges are usually faced with parties giving contradictory oral evidence and the difficult job of choosing between them, so documentary evidence which supports one account rather than the other is very helpful. It is often a good idea to take photographs in preparation for the case. For example if you are making a claim against a builder who you say has done bad work or you have been physically injured then having a photograph of things like the bad work, the injury and the scene of the accident will not only improve your credibility but may also help the judge to form a clearer picture of what went on and what is at issue. You can also use or draw up plans or maps to help you explain what happened. This is particularly useful in disputes about road accidents. It may save time if you can get your opponent to agree in writing before the hearing that your plans are accurate.

Other Physical Evidence & Site Visits. In addition to documents you can use other physical evidence to support your claims. For example if the dispute is about reasonably small and portable goods you could take the goods in question, or a sample, along to the small claims track to show that they are faulty in some way. In some circumstances the district judge may want to visit the scene of the accident or the place where unsatisfactory work was done, or to go and see an object which cannot be brought to the court. This is known as a site visit and both claimant and the defendant will be given notice in advance and the opportunity to attend.

Expert Evidence. This is required when it is necessary to decide a question that requires specialist or technical knowledge that the district judge is unlikely to have. For example, a surveyor may give an opinion on building works and a doctor will be a suitable expert in personal injury cases. When a matter calls for expert evidence only a suitably qualified person can give it. This does not necessarily mean that they must have formal qualifications although these are usually expected and it may be difficult to satisfy a judge that a witness is an expert if he does not have formal qualifications. You can claim from the defendant (or the claimant), with the judges permission up to £200 for cost of an expert report.

To find an expert you can contact the relevant professional or trade association and ask for a recommendation or a Citizens Advice Bureau or Trading Standards Officer may be able to help you find a suitable person. It is important not to use an expert you already have close connections with such as a relative or friend because the district judge is likely to give less weight to the evidence of an expert who is not entirely independent.

When you have found a suitable expert ask him to write a report. Explain clearly what you want and what is at issue. This will ensure he answers the important questions and also that he does not do unnecessary work which will increase your costs. It may be possible for both you and your opponent to minimise your expenses by agreeing to use the same expert. In which case you should agree in advance what questions you want the expert to answer and what evidence he will see.

Another alternative is for you to ask the court to appoint an expert to act as the district judge in place of the district judge. In such circumstances you and your opponent would share the costs. If you already have a pre-small claims track appointment you can request that the district judge agree to this procedure at that hearing. Alternatively you can apply on Form N244 and you will be given an appointment. Remember to give copies of expert reports to your opponent ant to the court before the small claims track date in accordance with the courts directions.

SPECIAL CASES-Road Traffic Accidents, Personal Injury etc.

The small claims track is available to minor personal injuries and claims of more complex nature than a simple money claim. This is not an invitation to take on more than you understand and in appropriate circumstances you should take advice before rushing in with an ill-prepared claim. A more difficult case would obviously require a more detailed understanding of the evidence required to succeed.

The Burden of Proof

It is the claimant who brings the case to court and who makes allegations about the defendant or his conduct and it is for the claimant to establish that these claims are true. In legal terms it is said that he bears the burden of proof, on a practical level both the claimant and the defendant can be subject to the "onus of proof". This means that when the claimant has made a plausible allegation and substantiated his claims, for example producing evidence that goods were delivered but not paid for then the onus is on the defendant to give an answer or give an explanation. The defendant might produce evidence of payment. This would then put the onus of proof back on the claimant. The claimant could allege that the payments were for other invoices and so on. Because the claimant bears the burden of proof, if at the end of the hearing the district judge finds that the claimant's and the defendant's arguments are of equal strength he must decide in favour of the defendant and dismiss the claim form. When he is making a counterclaim the defendant bears the burden of proof in respect of this part of the case.

The Standard of Proof

It is unlikely that either party will be able to prove their case with 100% certainty but this is not required. In order to discharge the burden of proof the claimant (or in a counterclaim the defendant) must show he is right "on the balance of probabilities". This means that the district judge must be satisfied that what he is claiming is more likely than not to be correct. The criminal standard of proof, that a case must be proved "beyond reasonable doubt" does not normally have any application in small claims.

What You Must Prove

At the hearing the claimant must prove each of the statements made in his particulars of claim, which amount to establishing liability, and the level of loss suffered; because if he is successful, the court will award damages to compensate him for his loss, not to punish the defendant. The claimant does not have to prove any of the particulars that are admitted by the defendant in his defence. It is also the claimant's responsibility to prove that the defendant received the claim form.

This is relevant when the defendant does not attend the hearing or attends but denies service, but it is not relevant when the defendant has returned one of the forms of admission, defence and counterclaim. The court will normally assume due service if the claim form is not returned by the post office. Likewise, the defendant must prove all of the allegations he makes in the counterclaim and the level of loss he may have suffered. He should also bring any evidence available to him which disproves or undermines any of the claimant's claims in the particulars of claim, or which supports the defendant's alternative account of events.

The Rules of Evidence

The rules of evidence that normally govern what evidence is admissible, which means what the judge will consider and take into account, do not apply to small claims.

Representation

The small claims procedure is designed with the intention that people will be able to conduct their own case and legal representation should not usually be necessary. Consequently you are allowed to have a lay representative to state your case for you, perhaps a friend or relative who feels more confident about speaking to the judge. A lay representative cannot be heard if the person he represents does not attend the hearing and the district judge has the right to exclude him for misconduct. A Limited company may be represented by a director.

Parties to a small claim are also entitled to employ a solicitor if they wish. However they will be unable to recover the cost of legal representation from their opponent if they are successful and so they will have to pay the costs themselves. Legal aid is not normally available for representation in small claims. If a party is unable to properly represent themselves in a small claim, for example as a result of a physical disability, poor sight, pronounced stammer or inability to read, these circumstances can be taken into account by the district judge when deciding whether or not the case should be automatically referred to small claims track or whether it should go to a county court trial for which legal aid may be available. If you feel you are unable to represent yourself inform the court well before the small claims track date and ask for a preliminary appointment for directions. You could also apply for legal aid on the grounds that your circumstances are exceptional. You may feel that your opponent is a better advocate or has instructed a solicitor. Inequality of representation can be worrying. However, the district judge will take a fairly active role to ensure that you are not unfairly disadvantaged. The district judge will be mindful of the overriding objective and the duty of the court to "deal with cases justly" and to "ensure that the parties are on an equal footing".

Chapter 9.

The Day in Court

___

You will receive notification of the date, time and place set for the small claims track hearing from the court when the case has been allocated to the small claims track. If you have not been there before allow plenty of time to find the court. You may wear what you wish but it is a good idea to dress smartly to make a favourable impression on the district judge. Bring the originals and spare copies of all the documents and the evidence you want to use at the hearing even though you have already sent copies to the court and you opponent.

When you arrive at court you will find a list of the days cases on a notice board. Check that your case is listed and inform the usher that you have arrived. The usher will know if your opponent has arrived, and if he is represented by a solicitor.

Unless you have a relatively long time estimate such as a full day, cases are usually listed in blocks. For example, a number of cases will be listed for 10.00am and 2.00pm and will be heard in order. This means you are likely to have to spend some time waiting around before the hearing. This gives you an opportunity to check that your opponent has received all the documents you or the court have served on him, and if he has not let him have a look at a copy. The waiting period could also give you an opportunity to settle the dispute if you consider it worthwhile, but beware of accepting an unfavourable settlement because of pre-hearing nerves. If you do achieve a compromise the judge will most likely approve it at the hearing and issue a consent order. When it is your turn to be heard the usher will show you into the judge's room. The judge will usually be sitting at the end of a long table. You and your opponent will sit on either side. The judge will not be wearing a wig or gown and should be addressed as "Sir or Madam". Ask the judge if he would prefer the witnesses to wait outside and be called in when required, or if they may sit in on the full hearing. Only the people involved in the case will present, although in practice small claims hearings are now open to the public. Evidence is not given on oath unless the district judge directs that it should be. Because it is the claimant who has brought the case to the small claims track and it is the claimant who has made allegations or claims against the defendant it is usual for the claimant to begin by presenting his case at the hearing. The defendant will then have an opportunity to respond.

How to Present Your Case - The claimant

- Ask the judge if he or she has all the documents in the case such as the claim form, defence, expert's reports and witness statements. If you have filed a witness statement ask the judge to read it

- Take the judge through the list of points you have prepared or the particulars of claim to explain your case. Identify what the defendant has admitted in the defence. This should give the judge a clear idea of what is at issue thus what he is being asked to decide.

- Having given an outline of your case, introduce the evidence you have to support it. This may include your own oral evidence, documents and possibly witnesses, although this is not essential.
- You, the judge and your opponent will all have an opportunity to question your witnesses. You will also be able to question your opponent and his witnesses.Except when you are questioning witnesses you should address your remarks to the judge. Avoid getting involved in any direct argument with your opponent.
- You may feel more confident in presenting your case if you have prepared and filed a witness statement yourself. You could then refer to your own statement when speaking to the district judge or answering questions

How to Present Your Case- The defendant

- You will probably have to wait while the claimant presents his claims against you to the judge. This may be very frustrating but do not interrupt or speak over your opponent. You will have an opportunity to put your side of the story later on.
- When the claimant is speaking make a note of any important point he makes. For example if there is something you would like to question him about later or a fact that has not emerged previously.
- After the claimant has spoken you will have the opportunity to present your defence. Use the notes you have prepared or your defence form to help you as you tell the judge all the important points.

- Try to respond to what the claimant has said.
- You will have an opportunity to call your witnesses and question them as well as an opportunity to question your opponent and his witnesses.
- If you have filed a Counterclaim this must be presented as though you were a claimant.
- You may feel more confident in presenting your case if you have prepared and filed a witness statement yourself. You could then refer to your own statement when speaking to the district judge or answering questions.
- Whether you are a claimant or a defendant it is in your own best interests to remain calm and courteous throughout the hearing.

Small Claims are Informal

The description outlined above makes the hearing seem rather formal. In practice, the judge may intervene and ask questions and the hearing will "ebb and flow" as the judge seeks to extract relevant information from both sides.

As the hearing may move on quickly, it is important to be familiar with the details of your claim or defence and to "put the record straight" when any detail is ignored or misunderstood.

Failure to Attend

If the claimant fails to attend, the judge could decide that there is no case to answer and dismiss the claim form. In such a case, the claimant could apply for judgement to be set aside if grounds exist. If the defendant fails to attend, the judge could enter judgement for the claimant or decide that there is no case to answer and dismiss the claim form.

If you find you are going to be unable to attend contact the court immediately to seek an adjournment.

Judgement

The District Judge may give reasons as briefly or simply as the nature of the case allows. Judgement will normally be given orally at the hearing but the decision may be given later, either in writing or at another hearing.

A reasoned decision

The judgement will contain the result of the case and brief reason for the decision. The detail in the decision will be proportionate to nature of the case, and the reasons given may be brief.

The decision will be reasoned but the judge must produce a written note of the reasons for the decision only if there was no recording or if the case was decide without a hearing under rule 27.10 or if either side notified the court that they did not propose to attend the hearing.

The District Judge's reasons will be considered by the Circuit Judge in the event of an appeal-if a reasonable note has been made that this may save the cost of a transcript of a judgement.

Costs and witness expenses

Decision on what expenses and costs are to be allowed, are taken after the award has been given and the District Judge will make a note of the sums awarded. The parties and their representatives should have their calculators ready, and be prepared to assist the district judge with interest calculations, witness expenses and arithmetical calculations.

Time to pay

If the loser needs time to pay the sum awarded, the District Judge will consider whether the judgement should be paid in instalments. If it is to be paid in one lump sum, the District Judge will decide when the payment is to be made. If no time period is set then judgement must be paid in full within 14 days. Note that if the loser is granted time to pay then the instalment order is registered as a judgement in the Register Of County Court Judgement.

Even if the District Judge does not give the loser time to pay at the hearing, an application can be made at a later date. The party requesting time to pay contacts the court and the staff will send them a form to complete enabling them to set out their income and liabilities, the court staff then work out an appropriate rate of payment using standard guidelines, the debtor and the creditor are both notified of the rate of payment which has been determined. If either the judgement debtor or creditor is unhappy with the rate determined by court, the matter is, at their request, referred to the District Judge who can confirm the order or set it aside and make a new order as they see fit, the judgement creditor does not have to accept a payment by instalments, for example, if the debtor has assets which could be sold to meet the debt then the District Judge may, at the request of the judgement creditor, set aside the instalment order.

Permission to appeal

The loser can ask the District Judge at the end of the hearing for permission to appeal. No formalities or fee is involved. If the request is refused, this does not affect the loser's right to make an application for permission to appeal to the circuit judge within 21 days of the hearing. Permission to appeal will be given only if the appeal has a real prospect of success. The District Judge will inform the parties that any further request to appeal must be made to the Circuit Judge who will hear any appeal. There is also a procedure to set aside a judgement given in the absence of one of the parties. If a party had a good reason for not attending and their case had a reasonable prospect of success, the District Judge may allow a rehearing.

Grounds for appeals

The grounds for appeal are limited, permission to appeal is required and the appeal is not usually a rehearing but a review of the decision of the District Judge. The appeal court (not to be confused with the Court of Appeal) will allow an appeal where the decision of the District Judge was wrong, or unjust because of a serious procedural, or other irregularity in proceedings in the lower court, the Circuit Judge will only interfere with a decision if it is wrong. This is not the same as a decision with which the loser disagrees.

Timeframe for appeals

Within 21 days of the decision	Appellant (person making appeal) must lodge notice of appeal (including application for permission to appeal if not granted by the District Judge at the hearing

Within 7 days of the appellant filing notice of appeal	Appellant must serve a copy of the notice of appeal on the other side (no need to serve the notice until permission to appeal has been given)
Within 14 days of the respondent being notified of the appeal	Respondent may lodge notice of appeal.

Paperwork for the appeal

Where the appeal relates to a claim allocated to a Small Claims track the appellant must file the following documents with the appellants notice:

1) A sealed copy of the order being appealed

2) Any order giving or refusing permission to appeal, together with reasons for that decision.

The form N164 must be properly completed to include all the reasons for appeal. Special permission will be needed to rely on any ground that is not included in the form N164. The form is lengthy but has helpful notes to aid completion. The N164 must be accompanied by a sealed copy of the order giving permission to appeal (if granted) and a "suitable record" of the District Judges reasons for the decision appealed against.

*****

Chapter 10.

Enforcing the Judgement

In this chapter the judgement debtor is referred to as the defendant but judgement debtors can also be claimants who have lost a counterclaim. Once you have obtained judgement on the claim or counterclaim no further action is required so long as the damages are paid. However judgement debtors do not always comply with the court's order to pay lump sum and may fall into arrears with payments to be made by instalments, in which case you have a number of options and can ask the court for any of the following:

A Warrant of Execution
This gives a bailiff the authority to visit the defendant's home or business and try to collect the money you are owed or to take goods to sell at auction. You can ask the bailiff to recover the whole amount or alternatively you can ask for part of the debt for example one or more instalments, or a minimum of £50.

You cannot normally ask for a part warrant if you originally asked for the judgement to be paid in one amount. A fee will be charged and this will be added to the amount you are owed by the defendant. The fee will not be refunded if the bailiff is not able to get anything from the defendant.

To request a warrant of execution, fill in form N323 and send it to the court. If you would like confirmation that the warrant has been issued you must also enclose a stamped address envelope. The court will send the defendant a notice to let him know that a warrant has been issued and that he must pay what is owed within seven days. If he complies the court will send the money on to you. If he does not the bailiff will call at his address within 15 working days of the warrant being issued to collect payment or take goods. The cost of taking and selling such goods will be deducted from the amount they raise when they are sold and then you will be sent your money.

There are limits placed on the type of goods a bailiff may take. He cannot take any items which are necessary for the basic domestic needs of the defendant and his family such as clothing or bedding or any items he requires to do his job or carry on his trade such as tools and vehicles. All property seized must belong to the defendant which means the bailiff cannot take goods which the defendant has on hire purchase, lease or which are rented, or which belong to someone else, such as the defendant's spouse. The bailiff may only take goods likely to fetch money at auction.

The defendant is entitled to ask that the warrant be suspended, in which case you will have a number of options. You can agree to the suspension of the warrant and accept the defendant's offer of payment, or agree to the suspension and ask that he pay more than the amount he has suggested. This would mean that a court officer would decide how much the defendant can afford to pay. Finally you can say that you do not agree to the suspension of the warrant and a hearing will be arranged.

If you object to the court officers decision about how much the defendant should pay fill in form N244 saying why you object and return it within sixteen days of the date of the postmark shown on the envelope the new order came in. A hearing will be arranged where a district judge will decide what the defendant should pay. If the warrant is suspended but the defendant still does not pay you can use form N445 to ask the court to reissue the warrant. There is no fee for doing this. If the bailiff was unable to recover any money or goods from the defendant and you have further information which means you think he should be able to then you can also reissue the warrant in these circumstances. For example, if you have a new address for the defendant or you can give details of an item the defendant owns and which would be worth selling use form N445 to inform the court.

A warrant lasts for one year. If you have still not received payment near the end of that time you should apply to extend the life of the warrant before the year ends otherwise you will have to ask for another warrant and a fee will be charged.

An Attachment of Earnings Order

If the defendant is in employment, he still owes you over £50 and he is behind with his payments you may be able to get an attachment of earnings order against him. This means the court will receive payments direct from the defendant's employer either monthly or weekly, depending on how he is paid and then will pass the money on to you.

To request an attachment of earnings order fill in form N55 and send it to the office of the defendant's local court with the fee.

If your judgement was obtained in another court you should first write to that original court, explain that you want an attachment of earnings order and ask that the case be transferred.

The defendant's local court will give you a new case number and you can then send in the request form N55 and the fee. Enclose a stamped address envelope if you would like confirmation that your request is being dealt with. The court will tell the defendant to pay the money owed or to fill in a form giving details of his income, expenditure and employment. A court officer will then decide how much the defendant can afford to pay having made allowance for what he needs to live on. The order will then be sent to the defendant's employer telling him what and when he should pay.

If you are not happy with the court officer's decision you can use form N244 to ask for a district judge to decide what the defendant can afford to pay. You must say why you object to the decision and return the form within sixteen days of the date of the postmark shown on the envelope which the attachment of earnings order came in. A hearing will then be arranged.

The defendant is entitled to ask that the order should be suspended and that he should be allowed to make payments directly to you. If the order has been suspended and the defendant still does not pay, use form N446 to request re-issue of the process so that the court will send the order to his employer. No fee is charged for this.

You cannot obtain an attachment of earnings order against a defendant who is in the army, navy or air force or is a merchant seaman, a firm or limited company. Nor can you obtain one against a defendant who is self-employed or unemployed. If the defendant is on a very low wage it might not be possible for the court to make such an order. If the defendant has found new work after a period of unemployment during which the order had lapsed you can use form N446 to ask the court to send the attachment of earnings order to the new employer.

A Garnishee Order

If you have obtained a judgement for more than £25 the court can order a person who owes the defendant money or who holds money on their behalf to pay you as much as is needed to cover the balance on your judgement, or if there is not sufficient to pay you as much as they have or owe. A garnishee order can apply to most debts but is normally used to obtain money from a defendant's bank or building society accounts. You should fill in form N349 giving the name and address of the person who owes the defendant money or the name and branch of the defendant's bank if you know it. The form must then be sworn on oath. This can be done before a court officer at any county court free of charge or before a solicitor who will charge you a small fee.

There will not be a hearing. A district judge will consider your application. If he decides to grant the order the court will send a garnishee order nisi to the person who owes or holds the money for the defendant. This person is known as the garnishee. This order will freeze the account. You will be sent a copy and the defendant will also be sent one seven days later.

Before the money is paid to the claimant the defendant and the garnishee will have the opportunity to tell the court if there are any good reasons why the garnishee order nisi should not be made absolute. For example the money really belongs to someone else or the account is overdrawn. If they do not have a reason the court will make a garnishee order absolute which will mean the garnishee has to pay the money to the claimant.

The order only freezes the money that was credited to the defendant on the date when the bank or person received the order. It does not cover money paid in later. Therefore it is a good idea to try and have it served when they are likely to have as much money as possible for example at the beginning of the month if that is when their salary is paid.

A Charging Order & Order for Sale

If the defendant does not have identifiable income or money for you to claim but does own property such as a house (either freehold or leasehold) or something such as bonds, stocks and shares, you can obtain a charging order over this property. The effect would be that you would have a right to part of the value of the property and when it is sold you will receive your money.

To obtain a charging order you must prove that the debtor owns the property. In the case of land this means obtaining "Office Copy Entries" from HM Land Registry for which you will need to complete a "public Index Map" search to find out the title number of the land. This order provides security for the debt and is equivalent to a mortgage. The order must be registered at HMLR to be effective against land.

Unlike the other types of enforcement proceedings there is no application form for a charging order. You should therefore use the general application form N244 supported by evidence i.e. a witness statement saying that the defendant owes you money and giving the details of the court order. The court fee is £50 although this should be checked. You should also say that the debt is a result of a judgement and give the date, case number and details of the judgement. State what the outstanding balance of the debt is then send the affidavit to the court with the document from the land registry and the fee.

Once you have a charging order you can ask the court to order the defendant to sell his property to pay the debt. This is a separate procedure under CPR Part 8 using form N208. You will therefore issue separate proceedings for a fixed date hearing (i.e. default judgement is not available) and pay another fee. In practice it is difficult to obtain such an order. The court is unlikely to order the sale of a valuable property or family home to pay a small debt. You are likely to find that the defendant's home is jointly owned with his or her spouse. Even if they are not registered as a legal owner a husband or wife can have rights over a house known as a "beneficial interest" which could stop you obtaining an order for sale. Furthermore the property is likely to be mortgaged and the mortgagee may well oppose the sale. You should take advice before applying for a charging order and especially before applying for an order for sale because these procedures can be complicated and costly.

Oral Examination

This is not a method of enforcement but is a means of finding out information about the defendant to enable you to decide if he is able to pay you and which method of enforcement would be most appropriate. You can request an oral examination by filling in form N316 and sending it to the defendant's local court with the fee. If you obtained your judgement in a different court you must write to that original court asking for the case to be transferred and then send your form and fee in once this has been done. If the defendant is a company you can request an oral examination of one of the directors. You can find out who the directors are by contacting Companies House. The case should be transferred to the court nearest the director's home or business address rather than the one nearest to the company's registered office.

The court will send the defendant a form telling him when to attend court and instructing him to bring any documents concerning his finances. The court may also send out a questionnaire for the defendant to complete prior to the hearing.

You will be notified of when the examination is to take place. Check whether you are required to attend. If you cannot but you have specific questions that you would like the defendant to be asked write to the court and ask that they be included in the examination. You will receive a copy of the defendant's answers after the examination.

If the defendant fails to attend, the examination will normally be adjourned and rescheduled for a new date. If this happens you may have to pay the defendant's reasonable travelling expenses to attend on the new date, known as "conduct money". The defendant is entitled to ask you for this at any time up to seven days before the date fixed for the adjourned examination. It is important that you write to the court just prior to the examination (no more than four days beforehand) to let them know that you have paid a reasonable amount for travelling expenses or that the defendant has not asked you for conduct money. If you have paid his expenses and the defendant fails to attend that amount will be added to what he owes you. An order to attend an adjourned oral examination must be served personally by a bailiff. If the defendant fails to attend the judge can issue a warrant for his arrest provided that he is satisfied the defendant knew of the examination. The bailiff will then arrest the defendant and bring him to the court to be examined. The court will send you a copy of his answers.

Third Party Debt Order

A third party debt order is an order which freezes money held by a person or organisation such as a bank, which might otherwise be paid to the defendant against whom you have a judgement. The person or organisation that is holding the money is referred to as the "third party". A third party debt order was previously known as a "garnishee order". A third party debt order is commonly used by a judgement creditor where the debtor has a bank account. It is usual for small businesses to keep copies of cheques they receive from customers. It is still possible to apply for a third party debt order if you don't have the debtor's bank account number, but you must at least have the name of the bank and branch where the account is held. The money held by the third party must be held solely for the debtor. You cannot, for example, apply for third party debt order against a joint bank account unless the judgement debt is against both account holders.

The timing of an application for a third party debt order is crucial. If you are applying for an order against the debtor's bank account, it takes affect on the day it is received by the third party and applies to money in the account on that day. So if you have an idea of when the debtor may receive money into the account, such as from their wages, it would be sensible to time the application so that the order will be received by the bank shortly after the money has gone into the account. Although you can try and select the right time for the application, it is still a very hit and miss affair. The order could be served one day before the account receives £1 million but the order would not be applied to that sum! The judgement creditor is therefore taking a gamble but it is hoped that there will be something in the account to make the application worthwhile.

To apply for a third party debt order, form N349 must be completed and sent to the court with the appropriate court fee.

The information required on form N349 is:

- The judgement debtor's name and address
- The total amount of the judgement debt and the amount still owing
- The name and address of the third party which must be in England and Wales
- The Head Office of the bank or building society. If known, you should give the name of the branch where the account is held, the branch address, the bank's sort code and the debtor's account number
- Whether or not you know of anyone else who has an interest in the same money

- Whether or not you have made any other applications for a third party debt order in respect of the same judgement
- The reason for your belief that the third party is indebted to the judgement debtor

The last point is probably the most important one. If a business has a copy of a cheque received from the debtor in respect of a previous payment, then the judgement creditor can state this as the reason for their belief and attach a copy of the cheque to the application.

If you want to serve the order yourself then you must tell the court when you send the application, otherwise the court will send it to the third party and judgement debtor. The creditor may wish to serve the order because it gives them control over the best time for the third party to receive it.

The application will be considered by a district judge and if satisfied with the information provided, he will make an interim third party debt order. The interim order will be sent to the third party and 7 days later will be served on the judgement debtor. This is to ensure that the third party freezes the money before the debtor becomes aware of the order. The interim order gives a date for a hearing when the district judge considers whether or not to make the other final. If the order is made final and the third party is a bank or building society, on receipt of the interim order they are required to carry out a search within 7 days to identify all accounts held by the judgement debtor. They must inform the court and the creditor of the account numbers, whether the account is in credit and if it is they must say whether there is sufficient money to cover the amount being claimed in the interim order.

It is important to remember that trying to attach money due from a bank to a debtor is not the only use of a third party debt order. If the judgement debtor is owed money by its customers, you could apply for third party debt order against that third party customer. The obvious difficulty here is that the judgement debtor may not give you sufficient or correct information to enable you to state in the application the reason why you believe the third party owes the judgement debtor the money.

Appointment of a Receiver
Receivership orders are made where it is not impossible to use any of the legal methods of enforcement. The order will authorise the receiver to receive money, rent and profits which the judgement debtor is entitled to because of his interest in specified property. When deciding whether or not to appoint a receiver the court will take into account the amount that is owed, the amount that is likely to be obtained by a receiver and the probable costs of the appointment. It is not a usual course of action for recovering debts arising out of a small claim.

Bankruptcy Proceedings
Non-payment of the debt could give you grounds to issue a bankruptcy petition against the defendant. The debt must exceed £750, it must be unsecured and the debtor must either be unable to pay or have no reasonable prospect of being able to pay.

Claimant's Obligations

If you have begun any of the enforcement proceedings and you receive full or partial payment from the defendant you must tell the court immediately.

Finding out about a debtor's assets

There are a number of sources of information available to members of the general public. The most important are set out in the table overleaf.

*

Organisation	About	Details	Cost
DVLC Swansea	Registered keeper of vehicle (this may not be the legal owner if the car is on finance-see HPI Equifax	Enquiries in writing only on form V888-phone 0300 123 1279	£5 but check current costs.
Electoral role	Discloses current and past residents at a given address	Local town hall and libraries upon personal application	Free
HPI Equifax	Will check if a vehicle is stolen, written off or is on finance	Enquiries answered over the phone on 0845 300 8005	£29.95 on phone
Land Registry	Provides the name of the registered owner of any house or land and details of mortgages	Local land Registry contact HM land Registry on 0844 892 1111	£4 but check
Local Bankruptcy County Court	Whether a bankruptcy petition has been issued against a judgement debtor	Contact the bankruptcy county court relevant to the debtors address	£5 but check
Companies House	Information about a company, including filed accounts	Crown Way Cardiff CF14 3UZ 0303 1234 500	Registered Office search is free

The Register of County Court Judgements

The judgement will be entered on the County Court Judgements Register and will remain there for six years. This may make it difficult to obtain credit, a mortgage or goods on hire purchase. Banks, building societies and credit companies search the Register.

If the full amount owed is paid within one month of the judgement date, a person can ask the court to take their name off the register. They will have to pay a fee of £3 (check for current rates) and give the court proof that the debt is paid, for example a letter from the claimant. The court will cancel the entry on the register and give a certificate of satisfaction to prove that the debt is paid within one month. If it is not paid within one month they can ask the court to mark the register "satisfied" when the full amount is paid. This will mean that anyone who searches the register will know the debt is paid and when the last payment was made. The debtor will receive a certificate of satisfaction but the entry will remain on register for six years. To obtain this send the fee of £3 and proof of payment.

****

Chapter 11.

The Costs of Small Claims

_____

County Court Fees

These are fees that must be paid to the court to commence and enforce your claim. When you issue a claim form and you are only claiming money the amount of the fee is determined by the size of your claim, as outlined below. (Always check figures before application as they may change). Fees correct as at April 2019.

County Court costs

1. Claims	Fee	Money claims online
Amount claimed is up to £300	£35	£25
Amount claimed is between £300 and £500	£50	£35
Amount claimed is over £500 but not over £1,000	£70	£60
Amount claimed is over £1,000 but not over £1,500	£80	£70
Amount claimed is over £1,500 but not over £3,000	£115	£105

£3,001-£5,000	£205	£185
AMOUNT CLAIMED IS OVER £5,000 BUT NOT OVER £10,000	£455	£410
Amount claimed is £10,000 but not over £100,000	5%	4.5%
Amount claimed is over £100,000 but not over £200,000	5%	n/a
Amount claimed is over £200,000	£10,000	n/a

See appendix for breakdown of all fees.

Recovering Costs From Your Opponent

Small claims are an exception to the usual practice where in general if you win your case your opponent pays you costs. In small claims even if you are entirely successful only a few of your possible expenses will be recoverable. They are :

- The costs which were stated on the claim form or which would have been on the claim form if the claim had been for a liquidated sum.

- Up to £200 in respect of the fees of an expert. Inclusive of VAT.

- Up to £260 for legal advice obtained to bring or defend a claim for an injunction, specific performance or similar relief. Inclusive of VAT.

- Up to £50 in respect of a party's or a witness's loss of earnings when attending a hearing.

- Any expenses which have been reasonably incurred by a party or witness in travelling to and from the hearing or in staying away from home

- The costs of enforcing the award.

- Such further costs as district judge may direct where there has been unreasonable conduct on the part of the opposite party in relation to the proceedings or claim that was made. An example of unreasonable conduct would be the fabrication of a wholly untruthful defence.

Injunction & Specific Performance

The provision of the county court rule which governs automatic reference to small claims track refers to actions where there is a "sum claimed" or "amount involved", thus it is arguable that if you are not claiming money but only seeking an injunction or specific performance your case should not be automatically referred to small claims track. If the case is not dealt with as a small claim this could mean it would be easier for you to claim legal aid, and more importantly that if you win your case you could recover costs from your opponent. Consequently if you are claiming a small amount in damages with your injunction it may actually save you money to forego the damages claim. Such consideration can be complex and difficult and you would put yourself at risk of paying your opponents costs if you lose so take advice from a solicitor on this question. Remember £260 spent in advance is recoverable even if the case proceeds as small claim.

Housing Matters

If you have a housing dispute for example, for nuisance or disrepair, you may be able to bring a claim in the magistrates court under the Environmental Protection Act 1990 as an alternative to small claims track. You can claim up to £5,000 in damages and get a nuisance order, which is equivalent to Specific performance. Legal aid is not available but if you are not successful you can claim your legal costs from your opponent.

..***

Glossary of terms

Allocation: The procedure by which a district judge decides if a case qualifies for the small claims track or some other track

Alternative Dispute Resolution: The form which both sides complete and send to the court to assist the District Judge when giving initial case management orders and when allocating the case to a track

Arbitration: A method of settling disputes by which the parties agree to determination by an arbitrator. This is commonly used in the settlement of commercial disputes.

Box work: The work done by a District Judge on a court file where there is no hearing and the parties are not present.

Case management: The process by which the District Judge controls the progress of a case by making orders and imposing sanctions

Circuit Judge: A County Court Judge senior in rank to a District Judge. Circuit Judges hear small claims appeals.

Claimant: The party who starts a small claims action.

Community Legal Service: The provider of legal services funded by the Legal Services Commission. They administer the replacement for the Legal Aid Fund, the Community Legal Services Fund.

Counterclaim: A claim by the defendant against the claimant.

Court Service: The government service responsible for running of all court in England and Wales (www.courtservice.gov.uk)

CPR (The Rules) The Civil Procedure Rules 1998, governing the action of the Small Claims Process.

Damages: A judgement entered because a defendant has not filed an acknowledgement or defence to claim within the specified time limit.

Defendant: The party against whom a claim is made.

Deputy District Judge: Part Time District Judge.

Detailed assessment of costs: When the costs of a case are decide after the case has been completed.

Directions: Orders made to govern the procedure in a case.

Disclosure: The process of each party notifying the others of any documents they intend to use at a hearing.

Disposal: A hearing after judgement when the amount due to the claimant is determined by the court.

District Judge: A member of the judiciary appointed to conduct business in the county court including the small claims court.

Evidence: Information given to the court to support a case.

Ex Parte application: An application made without giving notification to the other side. This term is obsolete under the CPR and the term "without notice" should be used.

Fast track: Case management track for cases up to £15,000 in value which can be heard in one day and which do not qualify for the small claims track.

Filing: Sending or taking a document to the court office.

Home court: The County court for the district in which the defendant's address for service, as shown on the defence, is situated.

Note that this is the solicitor's address if the defendant is legally represented.

Jurisdiction: The geographical area to which the Civil Procedure Rules apply. Note that Scotland and Ireland are not within the jurisdiction of the Rules.

Lay representative: Someone other than a lawyer exercising the limited rights of audience at the small claims court

Legal executive: A professional qualified under the rules of the Institute of Legal Representatives. Specially qualified legal executives can appear as advocates in open county court hearings.

Litigant in person: Someone who acts for themselves without using a lawyer representative.

Mediation: A voluntary, non-binding and private dispute resolution process in which a neutral person helps the parties try to reach a negotiated settlement the contents of which remain confidential and "without prejudice" unless or until a settlement is achieved.

Multi-track: Case management regime applicable to cases over £15,000 in value which does not qualify for the fast track.

Part 20 claim: Claims made in an action other than by a claimant-third party proceedings and counterclaims are types of Part 20 claims.

Part 36 offers and payments: Part 36 describes the rules which apply if a party wishes to make a formal offer to settle including the costs consequences.

Particulars of claim/defence: Details of a case-applies to a claim, defence or counterclaim.

Practice direction: The civil procedure rules are supported by formal guidance notes-in the case of small claims the practice direction includes the routine direction orders.

Pre-action protocol: This is to promote settlement before litigation.

Procedural judge: Any Judge who takes decisions about the procedure in a case. In the County court-this can be a District Judge or a Circuit Judge.

Right of audience: Being allowed to present a case in court on behalf of someone else or on one's own behalf.

Statement of Truth: Formal confirmation that the contents of a document are true.

Statements of case: Formal documents setting out the details of a case.

Stay: A court imposed halt on proceedings. A case can only continue if the stay is removed.

Strike out: This means that either the court ordering the end to a case or that certain written material be deleted so that it may no longer be relied upon

Summary assessment of costs: If the District Judge decides that any costs are payable in a small claims case, the amount will be decided there and then at the hearing.

Summary judgement: Procedure under Part 24 for obtaining a judgement without a full hearing.

Third party claim: A claim where the defendant wants to shift blame onto a party who was not brought into the action by the claimant.
Track: One of the special case management regimes under the Civil procedure Rules.

Unspecified claims: Claimant where the claimant leaves the amount of the claim to be determined by the court.

Without prejudice: Negotiations with a view to a settlement are usually conducted 'without prejudice' which means that the circumstances in which the content of those negotiations may be revealed to the court are very restricted.

****

Index

Appendix 1

1.Form N1 Claim Form

2.Notes for Claimant

3.Notes for Defendant-General

4.Enforcing a Judgement

5.Combined Certificate of Judgement

6.Court Fees (2020)

Claim Form

You may be able to issue your claim online which may save time and money. Go to www.moneyclaim.gov.uk to find out more.

In the	
Fee Account no.	
Help with Fees - Ref no. (if applicable)	H W F – ☐☐☐ – ☐☐

	For court use only
Claim no.	
Issue date	

Claimant(s) name(s) and address(es) including postcode

SEAL

Defendant(s) name and address(es) including postcode

Brief details of claim

Value

You must indicate your preferred County Court Hearing Centre for hearings here *(see notes for guidance)*

Defendant's name and address for service including postcode

	£
Amount claimed	
Court fee	
Legal representative's costs	
Total amount	

For further details of the courts www.gov.uk/find-court-tribunal.
When corresponding with the Court, please address forms or letters to the Manager and always quote the claim number.

	Claim No.	

Does, or will, your claim include any issues under the Human Rights Act 1998? ☐ Yes ☐ No

Particulars of Claim (attached)(to follow)

Statement of Truth

*(I believe)(The Claimant believes) that the facts stated in these particulars of claim are true.

* I am duly authorised by the claimant to sign this statement

Full name _____

Name of claimant's legal representative's firm _____

signed _____ position or office held _____

*(Claimant)(Litigation friend)   (if signing on behalf of firm or company)

(Claimant's legal representative)   *delete as appropriate*

Claimant's or claimant's legal representative's address to which documents or payments should be sent if different from overleaf including (if appropriate) details of DX, fax or e-mail.

Notes for claimant on completing a claim form

Before you begin completing the claim form

- You must think about whether alternative dispute resolution (ADR) is a better way to reach an agreement before going to court. The leaflet 'I'm in a dispute - What can I do?' explains more about ADR and how you can attempt to settle your claim.
- Please read all the notes which follow the order in which information is required on the form.
- Before completing this form, consider whether you might prefer to issue online www.moneyclaim.gov.uk
- If you are filling in the claim form by hand, please use black ink and write in block capitals.
- Copy the completed claim form and the defendant's notes for guidance so that you have one copy for yourself, one copy for the court and one copy for each defendant.
- If the claim is for a sum of money then you must send it to the County Court Money Claims Centre, PO Box 527, Salford, M5 0BY.
- If it is a High Court claim or is a claim for anything other than money you should send the form and the fee to a court office.
- You can get additional help in completing this form from the Money Claim helpdesk - phone 0300 1231372. If you need legal advice you should contact a solicitor or a Citizens Advice Bureau.

Further information may be obtained from Direct.gov.uk or from the court in a series of free leaflets.

Notes on completing the claim form

Heading

You must fill in the heading of the form to indicate the name of the court where you want the claim to be issued. If you want the claim to proceed in the County Court and it is for money only, you must enter 'County Court Money Claims Centre'.

The claimant and defendant

As the person issuing the claim, you are called the 'claimant'. Please enter your name and address. The person you are suing is called the 'defendant'. Please enter their name.

You must provide the following information about yourself and the defendant according to the capacity in which you are suing and in which the defendant is being sued.

Providing information about yourself and the defendant

full address including postcode

You should provide the address including postcode for yourself and the defendant or its equivalent in any European Economic Area (EEA) state (if applicable).

If an address does not have a postcode you will need to ask the judge for permission to serve the claim with this information missing. There is no additional fee for this, but the court will not allow your claim to be served without the postcode, unless you have permission from the judge.

When suing or being sued as:-

an individual:

You must enter his or her full name where known, including the title (for example, Mr., Mrs., Ms., Dr.) and residential address postcode and telephone number. Where the defendant is a proprietor of a business, a partner in a firm or an individual sued in the name of a club or other unincorporated association, the address for service should be the usual or last known place of residence or principal place of business.

Where the individual is:

trading under another name

you must enter his or her full unabbreviated name where known, and the title by which he or she is known and the full name under which he or she is trading, for example, 'Mr. John Smith trading as Smith's Groceries'.

suing or being sued in a representative capacity you

must say what that capacity is for example, 'Mr Joe Bloggs as the representative of Mrs Sharon Bloggs (deceased)'.

suing or being sued in the name of a club or other unincorporated association add the words 'suing/ sued on behalf of' followed by the name of the club or other unincorporated association.

an unincorporated business - a firm

In the case of a partnership (other than a limited liability partnership) you must enter the full name of the business followed by the suffix 'a firm' for example, 'Bandbox - a firm' and an address including postcode for service. This may either be one of the partners residential addresses or the principal or last known place of business of the firm.

a company registered in England and Wales or a Limited Liability Partnership

In the case of a registered company or limited liability partnership, enter the full name followed by the appropriate suffix (for example, 'Ltd'.) and an address including postcode which is either the company's registered office or any place of business in the UK that has a connection with the claim e.g. where goods were bought.

orporation (other than a company)
ter the full name of the corporation and any suffix
d the address including postcode in the UK which is
her its principal office or any other place where the
rporation carries on activities and which has a
nnection with the claim.

**overseas company (defined by s744 of the
mpanies Act 1985)**
ter the company's full name and any suffix if
propriate and address including postcode. The
dress must either be the registered address under
91 of the Act or the address of the place of business
ving a connection with the claim

der 18 write '(a child by Mr Joe Bloggs his litigation
end)' after the name. If the child is conducting
oceedings on their own behalf write
child)' after the child's name.

**patient within the meaning of the Mental Health
t 1983** write '(by Mr Joe Bloggs his litigation friend)'
er the patient's name.

ief details of claim
u must set out under **this** heading:
a concise statement of the nature of your claim
the remedy you are seeking e.g. payment of money

alue
you are claiming a **fixed amount of money**
'specified amount') write the amount in the box at
e bottom right-hand corner of the claim form against
mount claimed'.

you are not claiming a fixed amount of money (an
nspecified amount') under 'Value' write "I expect to
cover" followed by whichever of the following applies
your claim:

'not more than £10,000' **or**
'more than £10,000 but not more than £25,000' **or**
'more than £25,000'

you are **not able** to put a value on your claim, write
annot say how much I expect to recover'.

rsonal injuries
your claim is for 'not more than £5,000' and includes a
aim for personal injuries, you must also write 'My claim
cludes a claim for personal injuries and the amount I
pect to recover as damages for pain, suffering and loss
amenity is' followed by either:
'not more than £1,000' **or**
'more than £1,000'

Housing disrepair
If your claim is for 'not more than £5,000' and includes a
claim for housing disrepair relating to residential
premises, you must also write 'My claim includes a
claim against my landlord for housing disrepair relating
to residential premises. The cost of the repairs or other
work is estimated to be' followed by either:
- 'not more than £1,000' **or**
- 'more than £1,000'

If within this claim, you are making a claim for other
damages, you must also write:

'I expect to recover as damages' followed by either:
- 'not more than £1,000' **or**
- 'more than £1,000'

Preferred Court
You may be asked to send this claim to a court centre
that is not convenient for you to attend. If attendance is
required the court will transfer the case to make it easier
for one or all of the parties to attend. A list of County
Courts hearing centre can be found at:
hmctscourtfinder.justice.gov.uk State your preferred court
where indicated. The court will take it into account if
transfer is required.

Defendant's name and address
Enter in this box the title, full names, address and
postcode of the defendant receiving the claim form
(one claim form for each defendant). If the defendant is
to be served outside the UK or any other state of the
EEA, you may need to obtain the court's permission.

Legal representative's costs
These fixed sums may only be claimed where a legal
representative has been instructed to make the claim on
your behalf.

Particulars of claim
You must set out under this heading:
- a concise statement of the facts on which you rely
- a statement (if applicable) that you are seeking
  aggravated damages or exemplary damages
- details of any interest which you are claiming
- any other matters required for your type of claim as
  set out in the relevant practice direction

Statement of truth
This must be signed by you, your solicitor or your
litigation friend.

Where the claimant is a registered company or a
corporation the claim must be signed by either the
director or other officer of the company or (in the case
of a corporation) the mayor, chairman, president or
town clerk.

Address for documents
Please note that the service regulation provides that
cross-border service by any direct means including fax or
email is not permitted within the EEA.

Notes for defendant on replying to the claim form

Please read these notes carefully - they will help you decide what to do about this claim.
Further information may be obtained from the court in a series of free leaflets

- If this claim form was received with the particulars of claim completed or attached, you must reply within 14 days of the date it was served on you. If the words 'particulars of claim to follow' are written in the particulars of claim box, you should not reply until after you are served with the particulars of claim (which should be no more than 14 days after you received the claim form). If the claim was sent by post, the date of service is taken as the second business day after posting (see post mark). If the claim form was delivered or left at your address the date of deemed service will be the second business day (see CPR rule 6.14) after delivery.

- You may either:
    - pay the total amount i.e. the amount claimed, the court fee, and solicitor's costs (if any)
    - admit that you owe all or part of the claim and ask for time to pay, or
    - dispute the claim

- If you do not reply, judgment may be entered against you.

- The notes below tell you what to do.

- The response pack will tell you which forms to use for your reply. (The pack will accompany the particulars of claim they are served after the claim form).

- Court staff can help you complete the forms of reply and tell you about court procedures. But they cannot give legal advice. If you need legal advice, for example about the likely success of disputing the claim, you should contact a solicitor or a Citizens Advice Bureau immediately.

Registration of Judgments: If this claim results in a judgment against you, details will be entered in a public register, the Register of Judgments, Orders and Fines. They will then be passed to credit reference agencies which will then supply them to credit grantors and others seeking information on your financial standing. **This will make it difficult for you to get credit.** A list of credit reference agencies is available from Registry Trust Ltd, 173/175 Cleveland Street, London W1T 6QR.

Costs and Interest: Additional costs and interest may be added to the amount claimed on the front of the claim form if judgment is entered against you. In a county court, if judgment is for £5,000 or more, or is in respect of a debt which attracts contractual or statutory interest for late payment, the claimant may be entitled to further interest.

Your response and what happens next

How to pay

Do not bring any payments to the court - they will not be accepted.

When making payments to the claimant, quote the claimant's reference (if any) and the claim number.

Make sure that you keep records and can account for any payments made. Proof may be required if there is any disagreement. It is not safe to send cash unless you use registered post.

Admitting the Claim

Claim for specified amount

If you admit all the claim, take or send the money, including the court fee, any interest and costs, to the claimant at the address given for payment on the claim form, within 14 days.

If you admit all the claim and you are asking for time to pay, complete Form N9A and send it to the claimant at the address given for payment on the claim form, within 14 days. The claimant will decide whether to accept your proposal for payment. If it is accepted, the claimant may request the court to enter judgment against you and you will be sent an order to pay. If your offer is not accepted, the court will decide how you should pay.

If you admit only part of the claim, complete Form N9A and Form N9B (see 'Disputing the Claim' overleaf) and send them to the court within 14 days. The claimant will decide whether to accept your part admission. If it is accepted, the claimant may request the court to enter judgment against you and the court will send you an order to pay. If your part admission is not accepted, the case will proceed as a defended claim.

Claim for unspecified amount

If you admit liability for the whole claim but do not make an offer to satisfy the claim, complete Form N9C and send it to the court within 14 days. A copy will be sent to the claimant who may request the court to enter judgment against you for an amount to be decided by the court, and costs. The court will enter judgment and refer the court file to a judge for directions for management of the case. You and the claimant will be sent a copy of the court's order.

you admit liability for the claim and offer an
amount of money to satisfy the claim, complete
Form N9C and send it to the court within 14 days. The
claimant will be sent a copy and asked if the offer is
acceptable. The claimant must reply to the court within
14 days and send you a copy. If a reply is not received,
the claim will be stayed. If the amount you have offered
is accepted -

the claimant may request the court to enter
judgment against you for that amount.

if you have requested time to pay which is not
accepted by the claimant, the rate of payment will
be decided by the court.

your offer in satisfaction is not accepted -

the claimant may request the court to enter
judgment against you for an amount to be decided
by the court, and costs; and

the court will enter judgment and refer the court
file to a judge for directions for management of the
case. You and the claimant will be sent a copy of the
court's order.

Disputing the claim

If you are being sued as an individual for a specified
amount of money and you dispute the claim, the
claim may be transferred to a local court i.e. the one
nearest to or where you live or carry on business if
different from the court where the claim was issued.

If you need longer than 14 days to prepare your
defence or to contest the court's jurisdiction to try
the claim, complete the Acknowledgment of Service
Form and send it to the court within 14 days. This
will allow you 28 days from the date of service of the
particulars of claim to file your defence or make an
application to contest the court's jurisdiction. The court
will tell the claimant that your Acknowledgment of
Service has been received.

If the case proceeds as a defended claim, you and
the claimant will be sent a Directions Questionnaire.
You will be told the date by which it must be returned
to the court. The information you give on the form
will help a judge decide whether your case should be
dealt with in the small claims track, fast track or multi-
track. After a judge has considered the completed
questionnaires, you will be sent a notice of allocation
setting out the judge's decision. The notice will tell
you the track to which the claim has been allocated
and what you have to do to prepare for the hearing or
trial. Leaflets telling you more about the tracks are
available from the court office.

Claim for specified amount

If you wish to dispute the full amount claimed or
wish to claim against the claimant (a counterclaim),
complete Form N9B and send it to the court within
14 days.

If you admit part of the claim, complete the Defence
Form N9B and the Admission Form N9A and send
them both to the court within 14 days. The claimant
will decide whether to accept your part admission
in satisfaction of the claim (see under 'Admitting the
Claim - specified amount'). If the claimant does not
accept the amount you have admitted, the case will
proceed as a defended claim.

If you dispute the claim because you have already
paid it, complete Form N9B and send it to the court
within 14 days. The claimant will have to decide whether
to proceed with the claim or withdraw it and notify the
court and you within 28 days. If the claimant wishes to
proceed, the case will proceed as a defended claim.

Claim for unspecified amount/return of goods/non-money claims

If you dispute the claim or wish to claim against the
claimant (counterclaim), complete Form N9D and send
it to the court within 14 days.

Personal injuries claims:

If the claim is for personal injuries and the claimant
has attached a medical report to the particulars of
claim, in your defence you should state whether you:

- agree with the report or
- dispute all or part of the report and give your
  reasons for doing so or
- neither agree nor dispute the report or have no
  knowledge of the report

Where you have obtained your own medical report,
you should attach it to your defence.

If the claim is for personal injuries and the claimant
has attached a schedule of past and future
expenses and losses, in your defence you must
state which of the items you:

- agree or
- dispute and supply alternative figures where
  appropriate or
- neither agree nor dispute or have no knowledge of.

Address where notices can be sent

This must be either the business address of your
solicitor or European Lawyer or your own residential or
business address within the UK or in any other European
Economic Area state.

Statement of truth

This must be signed by you, by your solicitor or your
litigation friend, as appropriate.

Where the defendant is a registered company or a
corporation the response must be signed by either the
director, treasurer, secretary, chief executive, manager
or other officer of the company or (in the case of a
corporation) the mayor, chairman, president or town clerk.

Request for Warrant of Control

to be completed and signed by the creditor or their legal representative and sent to the court with the appropriate fee.

1. Creditor's name and address

In the

Claim no.

Fee Account no.

Help with Fees - Ref no. (if applicable)

H W F – ☐☐☐ – ☐☐☐

2. Name and address for service and payment (if different from above) Ref/Tel No.

3. Debtor's name and address

4. Warrant details

(A) Balance due at date of this request ←

(B) Amount for which warrant to issue

Issue fee

Legal representative's costs

Land Registry fee

TOTAL

If the amount of the warrant at (B) is less than the balance at (A), the sum due after the warrant is paid will be

I certify that the whole or part of any instalments due under the judgment or order have not been paid and the balance now due is as shown

Signed

Creditor (Creditor's legal representative)

Dated

IMPORTANT
You must inform the court immediately of any payments you receive after you have sent this request to the court

You should provide a contact number so that the bailiff can speak to you if they need to:

Daytime phone number: Evening phone number (if possible):

Contact name (where appropriate):

Debtor's phone number (if known):

If you have any other information which may help the bailiff or if you have reason to believe that the bailiff may encounter any difficulties you should write it below.

Combined certificate of judgment and request for writ of control or writ of possession

Creditor/Claimant

Debtor/Defendant

In the	
Claim No.	
Creditor's/ Claimant's Ref.	
Debtor's/ Defendant's Ref.	
Date	

Part 1

Date of judgment or order

Total amount of judgment *including any costs*

or

Details of order for possession *including any costs*

Total amount of interest accrued at the rate of _____ per day to date *(if any)*

I certify that the details I have given are correct and that to my knowledge there is no application or other procedure pending.

I request an order for enforcement in the High Court by

☐ Writ of Control

☐ Writ of Possession

I intend to enforce the judgment or order by execution against goods, and/or against trespassers in the High Court and require this Certificate for this purpose.

....

signed - (Creditor/Creditor's legal representative)
(Claimant/Claimant's legal representative)

....date

Part 2 *(for court use only)*

I certify that this is a true extract of the court record in this case.

Order for enforcement in the High Court by

☐ Writ of Control

☐ Writ of Possession

made on (date)..

....An Officer of the Court

Seal

Please Note:

This judgment or order has been sent to the High Court for enforcement by (Writ of Control) (Writ of Possession against trespassers) <u>only</u>.

The county court claim <u>has not been transferred</u> to the High Court. Applications for other methods of enforcement or ancillary applications <u>must</u> be made to the County Court hearing centre in which the judgment or order was made, unless the case has since been transferred to a different court, in which case it must be made to that court.

For further details of the courts www.gov.uk/find-court-tribunal. When corresponding with the Court, please address forms or letters to the Manager and always quote the claim number.

THE ACTION DEPARTMENT of the High Court is open between 10am and 4.30pm. All correspondence should be sent to the Court Manager, Action Department, Royal Courts of Justice, Strand, London WC2A 2LL

N293A Combined certificate of judgment and request for writ of fieri facias or writ of possession (04.14)

/ continued overleaf

rt 3

In the High Court of Justice

Queen's Bench Division at

Sent from the   County Court by

Certificate dated the   day of   )

High Court Enforcement Number

County Court Claim Number

Address of (Debtor)
(property of which possession is to be given)

Seal a Writ of (Control)(Possession) directed to the:

To: "_____, an
enforcement officer authorised to enforce writs of execution
from the High Court'.

Or,

'The enforcement officers authorised to enforce writs of
execution from the High Court who are assigned to the
district of [1] _____ in England and Wales'.

Note: If you have chosen this option you must send this writ to the
National Information Centre for Enforcement for allocation.

against_____

for: *(Complete A, B, C as approriate)*
A. the sum of:
         (a) debt   **£**
         (b) costs and interest   **£**
         (c) Subsequent costs   **£**
            (if any)

B. and interest thereon at ....% per annum from
the date of transfer and costs of execution

C. possession of

    and £   for costs.

Signed
Address for service
Date

HM Courts & Tribunals Service

EX50

Civil and Family Court Fees
From 3 August 2020

Important information

This leaflet sets out a selection of civil and family court fees. It is not the full list, neither is it the authority on fees. For a full list of fees charged in the civil and family courts please see the EX50AHMCTS on **hmctsformfinder.justice.gov.uk**

The full lists of all court fees are contained in Statutory Instruments (SIs) known as fees orders and can be found online at **www.legislation.gov.uk**

Please refer to Formfinder for a list of all court forms
http://hmctsformfinder.justice.gov.uk/HMCTS/FormFinder.do

If you are unsure which form you need you can search for your issue on www.gov.uk or get legal advice from a solicitor or Citizens Advice, www.citizensadvice.org.uk

The court fees set out in this leaflet apply to, and are the same in, both the High Court, County Court and the Family Court, unless otherwise stated. Your local court will be able to help you identify any fee not contained in this leaflet.

Time for payment of fees

Court fees are payable at the time you file any document or start any process needing a fee, unless otherwise stated.

Methods of payment

Courts accept payment by debit or credit cards, cash, postal orders or cheques, which should be made payable to '**HM Courts & Tribunals Service**'. If you pay by cheque and it is dishonoured, the court will take steps to recover the money. Non-payment will result in your case being stayed (delayed) or even struck out (dismissed).

You can pay by debit or credit card over the phone by contacting the court or providing your contact details for making payment and provide any paperwork required. Please do not send your bank details to the court.

What if I cannot afford to pay a court fee?

You may not have to pay a fee, or you may get some money off it if you only have a small amount of savings and investments, receive certain benefits or are on a low income. This is sometimes known as 'fee remission.'

You can apply for help with court and tribunal fees online at **www.gov.uk/help-with-court-fees** or through the 'EX160 Apply for help with fees' form and 'EX160A – How to apply for help with fees' guidance.

Refunds

If you have applied to issue a claim by post, and the defendant settles the dispute before your claim is processed by the court or business centre, you will be entitled to a refund as long as you have told us that the claim should not be issued.

If your case settles please email or phone the relevant County Court hearing centre or business centre. The contact details can be found at **www.gov.uk/find-court-tribunal**

You should keep a record of the fact that you have told us.

If your claim has already been issued, you can recover the cost of your court fee from the defendant.

Please do not cancel a cheque or card payment to HM Courts & Tribunals Service. Cancellation of a cheque or payment could result in us pursuing the fee from you as a civil debt.

HM Courts & Tribunals Service typically only refunds fees where the court has made a processing error, i.e. the court have processed a claim or application even though you have requested that it should not be processed.

Refunds will not be provided for any duplicate application or claim that is received at court due to it being sent via multiple channels (such as post and email) or multiple times. The Court Manager has the discretion to approve refunds that are the result of a genuine error.

If you want to apply for a fee refund, please write to the relevant County Court hearing centre or business centre (details can be found on Court and Tribunal Finder **www.gov.uk/find-court-tribunal**) explaining why you think you should have a refund. Applications should be made as soon as possible after payment of the fee.

Please note that fee refunds will not be provided for claims issued through MCOL or PCOL unless there has been a system error, i.e. where a fee has been charged twice.

Refunds requested under the fee remission scheme will not be provided in relation to fees paid on MCOL.

Online services

HM Courts & Tribunals Service has two internet based services: Money Claim Online (MCOL) for some money claims up to the value of £99,999.99, and Possession Claim Online (PCOL) for possessions concerning rent or mortgage arrears. You can use either of these simple, convenient and secure processes and pay a reduced fee online by debit or credit card.

For more information ask court staff or visit our websites:

www.moneyclaim.gov.uk

www.possessionclaim.gov.uk

Contents Page

Civil court fees

Family court fees

Civil court fees

Issuing claims

Money claims – Civil Fees Order 1.1-1.2

To issue a claim for money, the fees are based on the amount claimed, including interest. For Court Issued Claims, please round fractions of pence down to the nearest penny. Example: A Fee calculated as being £1050.5096 rounds down to a payable fee of £1050.50:

Value of your claim				Fee payable	
				Court issued claim	Filed via SDT/MCOL*
Up to	£300			£35	£25
Greater than	£300	but no more than	£500	£50	£35
Greater than	£500	but no more than	£1,000	£70	£60
Greater than	£1,000	but no more than	£1,500	£80	£70
Greater than	£1,500	but no more than	£3,000	£115	£105
Greater than	£3,000	but no more than	£5,000	£205	£185
Greater than	£5,000	but no more than	£10,000	£455	£410
Greater than	£10,000	but no more than	£200,000	5% of the value of the claim	4.5% of the value of the claim
Greater than	£200,000			£10, 000	N/a

* Maximum amount for Secure Data Transfer (SDT) or Money Claim OnLine (MCOL) £99,999.99

Secure Data Transfer is a secure system to enable customers issuing in bulk to upload and transfer data files directly from their systems to HM Courts & Tribunals Service systems.

Non-money claims

To issue a claim for possession – fees order 1.4

High Court possessions	£480
County Court possessions	£355
Possession Claims Online (PCOL)	£325

(PCOL can only be used for possessions concerning rent or mortgage arrears).

To issue a claim for something other than money or possessions (e.g. civil injunctions, gas injunctions, anti-social behaviour injunctions) the fees are based on where you start your claim - fees order 1.5

High Court (including possession claims)	£528
County Court	£308

If you file an application for a non-money claim (other than a claim for possession of land or recovery of goods) and a claim for damages, both court fees must be paid.

Example: County Court fee or High Court fee (fee 1.5 above) plus relevant money claim fee (the court issued claim fee 1.1 on page 5).

Certain non-money claims will attract the hearing fees set out on page 7. Check with the court to see if your case is affected.

Other fees associated with starting a claim

Issue proceedings against a party or parties not named in the proceedings – fees order 1.6	£55
Permission to issue proceedings – fees order 1.8(a)	£55

Please note, the fees in this section are not paid in respect of applications to commence proceedings under the Companies Act or in Insolvency proceedings. Instead, please see page 10.

Counterclaims and additional claims

- **Money claims** - the court fee payable (set out on page 5) is based on the value of the counterclaim or additional claims. If the original claim was issued in a court, the court issue fee applies. If the claim was issued through Money Claims Online (MCOL) or the County Court Business Centre (CCBC), the reduced MCOL fees apply.

- If you need to amend your claim you will need to make an application. Please refer to page 8 for general applications fees. The fee will depend on whether the claim has been served and therefore whether the application is on notice. If you amend the amount claimed you will need to pay the difference for the court fee payable as set out on page 5.

- **Non-money claims** - the court fee payable is based on where the original claim was made, either in the High Court or County Court. The court fees are set out above.

Costs proceedings

For court fees relating to the issue of costs only or cost assessment proceedings, go to pages 10 and 11.

General fees for civil proceedings

The fees on page 5, for issue of a claim, are payable by the claimant. The hearing fees below are payable by the claimant, unless the case continues on the counterclaim alone, in which case the hearing fees are payable by the defendant.

Hearing fees – fees order 2.1

Small Claim Track where the amount claimed is:

up to £300	£25
between £300.01 and £500	£55
between £500.01 and £1,000	£80
between £1,000.01 and £1,500	£115
between £1,500.01 and £3,000	£170
more than £3,000	£335

Please refer to the court leaflet EX306 – The Small claims track in the civil courts for further information.

Fast track claim	£545
Multi track claim	£1,090

Please refer to the court leaflet EX305 – The Fast Track and the Multi-Track in the civil courts for further information on tracked claims.

- You must pay to the court the hearing fee or file an application for Help with Fees by the date given in the order.

- Failure to pay the fee or make the appropriate application for Help with Fees will result in the claim/counterclaim being struck out with immediate effect without further order and the hearing removed from the list

- If your claim has been struck out, it will no longer exist. You may, if you wish, file an application to have the claim reinstated. However, please note that the application will itself attract a fee and, if the court permits the application to reinstate, that permission will be conditional on payment of the appropriate hearing fee or application for help with fees.

- The hearing will be vacated, a Counterclaim hearing fee is only payable by the defendant (if counterclaim acts alone).

- The hearing fee is non refundable. If parties settle before the hearing fee is due, the hearing fee will not be payable.

General applications – fees order 2.4-2.8

- Application on notice where no other fee is specified.	£255
- Application to set aside a County Court judgment.	£255
- Application by consent or without notice where no other fee is specified.	£100
- applications to vary (amend/change) or extend an injunction for protection from harassment or violence	£50
- applications for a payment out of funds deposited in court	£50

On/With notice means notification of the application to the other side, regardless of whether there is a hearing or not.

Without notice means no notification of the application to the other parties, regardless of whether there is a hearing or not.

If an application by consent or without notice/is refused and is ordered on notice the excess balance of the fee should be paid to the court to process the application on notice.

No fee is payable for an application by consent for an adjournment of a hearing if received by the court at least 14 days before the date of the hearing.

- Application to vary (amend/change) a judgment (or order), suspend enforcement or suspend a warrant of possession or stay a High Court Writ.   £14

- Application for a summons or order for a witness to attend court.   £21

- Application for a certificate of satisfaction/cancellation of a judgment debt.   £14

Bulk applications - An application without notice fee is charged for each case to substitute or change a parties name.

The only exception is CCBC cases where bulk applications are automated and therefore only one fee is payable per application with multiple cases.

These applications are not payable in respect of general applications to court under the Companies Act and Insolvency proceedings see page 10.

Appeals – fees order 2.2-2.3

Please refer to the court leaflet EX340 – I want to appeal - what should I do for further information.

On filing an appellant's notice or respondent's notice in the:

- High Court   £240
- County Court
  - Small claims track   £120
  - All other claims   £140

Other fees are payable in appeal proceedings where applications are made. These fees do not apply on appeals against a decision made in detailed cost assessment proceedings (see page 12).

Companies Acts and Insolvency proceedings
Companies Act 1985, Companies Act 2006 and Insolvency Act 1986
(High Court and county court)– fees order 3.1-3.12

Bankruptcy and company winding-up petitions

- Entering a petition to make someone who owes you money bankrupt (creditor's petition).   £280
- Entering a winding-up petition (companies only).   £280
- Any other petition where no other fee is specified.   £280

These are just the court fees. An additional amount, known as the Official Receiver's deposit, is payable at the same time as the court fee. The court processing your application will tell you how much the deposit is.

Note: Some insolvency proceedings are allocated to the multi-track and will attract the multi-track hearing fees set out on page 5. Check with the court to see if your case is affected.

Other applications

- Application under the Companies Acts or the Insolvency Act 1986 other than one brought by petition and where no other fee is specified (not payable when made in existing proceedings) - fees order 3.5   £280
- Application to convert a voluntary arrangement into a bankruptcy or winding up – fees order 3.6   £160
- Application on notice in existing insolvency or Companies Act proceedings where no other fee is specified – fees order 3.12   £95
- Application by consent or without notice in existing insolvency or Companies Act proceedings where no other fee is specified – fees order 3.11   £25
- Request for a certificate of discharge from bankruptcy – fees order 3.4(a)   £70

- Request for a copy of a certificate of discharge from bankruptcy
  – fees order 3.4(b)   £10

Bankruptcy searches

- On a general search in the records of the High Court for each
  15 minutes or part 15 minutes – fees order 10.3   £11

- On a search in person, including where a court officer searches the
  bankruptcy and companies records in the County Court   £45
  – fees order 3.13

Other civil court fees

Copy documents – fees order 4.1-4.2

If you ask the court to make copies of documents, receive or send a fax on
your behalf, or provide a copy of a document already provided:

- For between one and ten pages of any document.   £10

- For each subsequent page.   50p per page

- For copies of documents provided on computer disk or other
  electronic form.   £10

Costs-only proceedings – fees order 1.8(b)

Where parties have agreed a dispute without issuing a claim or petition,
but the issue of costs has not been agreed, either party can issue a claim
for costs only proceedings.

- Starting costs-only proceedings.   £55

Costs assessment proceedings – fees order 1.8(b)

Where a client is legally represented and there is a dispute over the amount
of costs payable to the solicitor, the client can make an application for the
costs to be assessed by the court.

- Application for an order under Part 3 of the Solicitors Act 1974 for the assessment of costs. £55

Determination of costs – fees order 5.1

On filing a request for a detailed assessment:

- Where the party who files the request is legally aided or funded by the Legal Aid Agency (LAA). £220

Where the following applications are made, the fee depends on the amount of costs being claimed:

- Filing a request for a detailed assessment where the party filing the request is not legally aided or funded by the LAA; or

- Request for a hearing date for the assessment of costs following an order under Part 3 of the Solicitors Act 1974

where the costs claimed are: – fees order 5.2

up to £15,000	£369
£15,000.01 – £50,000	£743
£50,000.01 – £100,000	£1,106
£100,000.01 – £150,000	£1,480
£150,000.01 – £200,000	£1,848
£200,000.01 – £300,000	£2,772
£300,000.01 – £500,000	£4,620
more than £500,000	£6,160

- Appeal against a decision made in detailed assessment proceedings – fees order 5.4 £231

- Request to issue a default costs certificate – fees order 5.3 £66

- Request or application to set aside a default costs certificate – fees order 5.5 £121

- Application for approval of a costs certificate payable from the Civil Legal Aid Fund (only applicable if the original request for detailed assessment was filed before 1 July 2013) – fees order 2.5(b)   £50

Civil Enforcement proceedings

If the court has ordered someone to pay you a sum of money or to return your goods, property or land, and they have not done so, you can issue enforcement proceedings.

Order to obtain information from a debtor

- To issue an application for an order for a debtor or other person to attend court to provide information – fees order 8.3   £55

- To request Bailiff service of an order for a debtor to attend court for questioning – fees order 8A.1   £110

Warrants – fees order 8.1-8.2 and 8.6

- To issue a warrant of control (recovery of a sum of money) via Money Claims Online or County Court Business Centre.   £77

- To issue a warrant of control (recovery of a sum of money) in any other case.   £110

- To issue a warrant of delivery (for goods).   £121

- To issue a warrant of possession (recovery of a property or land).   £121

- To request a further attempt to execute a warrant at a new address, except where a warrant has been suspended.   £33

Writs (High Court only) – fees order 7.1

- Sealing a writ of control (recovery of a sum of money).   £66

- Sealing a writ of delivery (for goods).   £66

- Sealing a writ of possession (recovery of a property or land).   £66

Where a warrant or writ of delivery or possession also includes a claim for money, there is no additional fee.

Attachment of earnings – fees order 8.7

- Application for an attachment of earnings order (a fee is payable for each defendant against whom the order is requested). £110

On a consolidated attachment of earnings order, a fee of 10p for every £1, or part £1, of money paid into court, is deducted from the money before it is paid out to the creditors.

Please refer to court leaflet *EX323 – Attachment of earnings for further information.*

Enforcing an award in the County Court – fees order 8.9

- Application for the enforcement of an award for a sum of money or other decision made by any court, tribunal, body or person other than the High Court or County Court or, in respect of the enforcement of an award for a sum of money, the First-tier Tribunal, Upper Tribunal, Employment Tribunal or Employment Appeal Tribunal. £44

Enforcing an award in the High Court – fees order 7.5

- Request or application: £66
    - to register a judgment or order; or
    - for permission to enforce an arbitration award; or
    - for a certificate or certified copy of a judgment or order for use abroad.

Charging order – fees order 8.4(b)

Please refer to the court leaflet *EX325 – Third party debt orders and charging orders for further information.*

- Application for a charging order.
  (A fee is payable for each charging order applied for). £110

Third party debt order – fees order 8.4(a)

Please refer to the court leaflet *EX325 – Third party debt orders and charging orders for further information.*

- Application for a third party debt order.
  (A fee is payable for each party against whom the order is requested). £110

Judgment summons – fees order 8.5

- Application for a judgment summons. £110

Certified Enforcement Agent

Application – fees order 1.5

- Other non-money fee for County Courts £308

For all Civil Magistrates fees please refer to the Magistrates' Courts fees order www.legislation.gov.uk

Family court fees

Not all courts can deal with family cases. You can find the full list of courts, and information about what work they do, online at **www.gov.uk/find-court-tribunal** or by phoning your local court.

Marriage and civil partnership proceedings

- Filing an application for a divorce, nullity or civil partnership dissolution – fees order 1.2 £550
- Filing an application for judicial separation – fees order 1.3 £365
- Filing an application for a second or subsequent matrimonial or civil partnership order with permission granted – fees order 1.5 £95
- Filing an answer to an application for a matrimonial or civil partnership order – fees order 1.6 £245
- Filing an amended application for a matrimonial or civil partnership order – fees order 1.5 £95
- Filing an application to start proceedings where no other fee is specified – fee order 1.1 £245
- Filing a Declaration as to marital status, parentage, legitimacy or adoptions effected overseas – fees order 1.3 £365

Financial orders

- Application for a financial order, other than by consent – fees order 5.4 £255
- Application by consent for a financial order – fees order 5.1 £50

Applications for injunctions

Family homes and domestic violence applications:

- Application for a non-molestation order.   No fee payable
- Application for an occupation order.   No fee payable

Please note only the respondent's first attempt to challenge a non-molestation order is free. Any further attempts require a fee of £95.

Forced Marriage and Female Genital Mutilation Protection Order applications

No fee is payable by an applicant to issue Forced Marriage or Female Genital Mutilation Protection Order proceedings or to apply to amend, vary or extend an order.

- Respondent's first attempt to challenge the order is free but any further application attracts a fee   £95

Children

The court leaflet 'CB1 - Making an Application – Children and the Family Courts' provides more information on the types of Children Act applications and who can make them. A selection of the more common applications are set out below:

Applications under the Children Act 1989 – fees order 2.1

- Any new applications under the Children Act 1989 to request permission to issue proceedings or for an order or directions to be made concerning the child(ren) e.g. Child Arrangements Order, Prohibited Steps Order, Specific Issue Order or Special guardianship order - with the exception of applications for care and supervision orders which are issued by Local Authorities.   £215

- An application for an enforcement order under the Children Act 1989 or an order for compensation for financial loss, due to the breakdown of a child arrangement order   £215

- Application to revoke, amend, extend or take action following the breach of an exisiting Children Act 1989 enforcement order   £95

There are only two instances in the family fees order where £245 is payable, Proceedings under the Children Act 1989 is not one of them. They are:

- Fee 1.1 of the family fees order - On filing an application to start proceedings where no other fee is specified. £245

- Fee 1.6 of the family fees order - On filing an answer to an application for a matrimonial or civil partnership order. £245

Applications to issue new proceedings under the Children Act 1989 are defined as any application for an order where there are no proceedings for the child(ren) currently being considered by the court. If proceedings under the Children Act 1989 are already being considered for the child(ren) the application fee for applications within proceedings will be charged. See the section headed 'Applications within proceedings' for further details.

Please note an application for enforcement should be made first with a fee of £215 and only thereafter an application for a breach with a fee of £95 can be made.

Adoption – fees order 3.1-3.3

- On an application for permission, or an order £170

One child or multiple siblings filed together is one fee of £170. If filed separately, and at different times, then a fee is payable of £170 each time.

- Application for a placement order (section 22) £455

One child or multiple siblings filed together is one fee of £455. If filed separately, and at different times, then a fee is payable of £455 each time.

- Revocation of placement fee £170

If you are issuing applications for siblings at the same time only one fee is payable.

Children Act and adoption applications

Where an application is made or permission is sought under two or more provisions of the Children Act 1989, or the Adoption and Children Act 2002, or the Children and Adoption Act 2006, only one fee is payable, and if the fees are different, the highest fee is paid.

Maintenance orders

Please see the family enforcement proceedings (pages 18 and 19) section for details of the fees applicable when applying for an order to enforce an order for the payment of money. If you wish to vary an existing Maintenance Order see the Applications within Proceedings section.

Applications within proceedings

- Application on notice where no other fee is specified – fees order 5.3   £155

- Application by consent or without notice where no other fee is specified, e.g application to vacate or adjourn a hearing – fees order 5.1   £50

    - **On/With notice** means notification of the application to the other side, regardless of whether there is a hearing or not.

    - **Without notice** means no notification of the application to the other parties, regardless of whether there is a hearing or not.

Appeals

On filing a notice of appeal:

- On filing an appeal notice from a district judge, one or more lay justices (Magistrates), a justices' clerk or an assistant to a justices' clerk, except appeal against decisions under the Children Act 1989 – fees order 6.1   £125

If you are issuing applications for siblings at the same time only one fee is payable.

- Of any provision of the Children Act 1989, except in relation to appeals for breach of or revocation of an enforcement order – fees order 2.3-2.4   £215

Family Request for service – fees order 15.1

- Request for service by a Bailiff for any document.   £45
- Request for bailiff service on an application for non-molestation, occupation, forced marriage or female genital mutilation orders made by the applicant or third-party applicant.   No fee payable

Other family fees

Copy documents – fees order 8.1-8.2

If you ask the court to make copies of documents, receive or send a fax for you, or provide a copy of a document already provided:

- For between one and ten pages of any document. £10
- For each subsequent page of the same document. 50p per page
- For copies of documents provided on computer disk or other electronic form. £10

Family Determination of costs – fees order 9.1-9.5

On filing a request for a detailed assessment:

- Where the party who files the request is legally aided or funded by the Legal Aid Agency (LAA). £94

Where the following applications are made, the fee payable depends on the amount of costs being claimed:

- Filing a request for a detailed assessment where the party filing the request is not legally aided or funded by the LAA; **or**
- Request for a hearing date for the assessment of costs following an order under Part 3 of the Solicitors Act 1974 where the costs claimed are:

up to £15,000	£335
£15,000.01 – £50,000	£675
£50,000.01 – £100,000	£1,005
£100,000.01 – £150,000	£1,345
£150,000.01 – £200,000	£1,680
£200,000.01 – £300,000	£2,520
£300,000.01 – £500,000	£4,200
more than £500,000	£5,600

- Appeal against a decision made in detailed assessment proceedings. £210
- Request to issue a default costs certificate. £60
- Request or application to set aside a default costs certificate. £110

Family Enforcement proceedings

If the court has ordered someone to pay you a sum of money or to return your goods, property or land, and they have not done so, you can issue enforcement proceedings.

Method of enforcement as the Court may consider appropriate - fees order 5.1

- Application in the family court for an order for such method of enforcement as the court may consider appropriate
£50

Order to obtain information from a debtor - fees order 12.1

- To issue an application for an order for a debtor or other person to attend court to provide information.
£50

- To request Bailiff service of an order for a debtor to attend court for questioning.
£100

Attachment of earnings - fees order 12.5

- Application for an attachment of earnings order (a fee is payable for each defendant against whom the order is requested).
£34

Charging order - fees order 12.3

- Application for a charging order. (A fee is payable for each charging order applied for).
£38

Judgment summons - fees order 12.4

- Application for a judgment summons.
£73

Third party debt order

- Application for a third party debt or garnishee order/Appointment of Receiver. (A fee is payable for each party against whom the order is requested) - fees order 12.2
£77

- Application for enforcement of a judgement or order - fees order 13.1
£100

Warrant of control fees

- Request for enforcement of a warrant at a new address - fees order 13.2   £30
- Issue for a warrant of possession or a warrant of delivery - fees order 13.3   £110
- To issue a warrant of control (recovery of a sum of money) - fees order 13.1   £100

Enforcement in the High Court - fees order 14.1-14.2

- Sealing a writ of control/possession/delivery   £60
- Request/application to register a judgment or order   £60

Searches - fees order 7.1-7.3

Index of decrees absolute or final orders

On a search of the index for any specified period of ten calendar years or the ten most recent years.

- Search of the national central index of decrees absolute/final orders   £65
- Search of the national central index of parental responsibility agreements   £45
- Search of any specific family court or District Registry index of decrees absolute/final orders   £45

The fee includes a copy of the agreement, if appropriate.

If you need this leaflet in an alternative format, for example in large print, please contact your local court for help.

If you have a disability that makes going to court or communicating difficult, please contact the court concerned and they will be able to help you.

You can find contact details for all our courts online at **www.gov.uk/find-court-tribunal**